The Michael Letters
of Rudolf Steiner

The Michael Letters of Rudolf Steiner

The Mission of Archangel Michael

First published in 2021 by Floris Books
© 2021 Estate of Charles Kovacs

The author has asserted his right under the Copyright Act 1988 to be identified as the Author of this Work

All rights reserved. No part of this publication may be reproduced without the prior permission of Floris Books, Edinburgh
www.florisbooks.co.uk

British Library CIP Data available
ISBN 978-178250-679-9
Printed and bound in Great Britain by Bell & Bain, Ltd

 Floris Books supports sustainable forest management by printing this book on materials made from wood that comes from responsible sources and reclaimed material

Contents

Foreword	7
1. At the Dawn of the Michael Age	9
2. The Condition of the Human Soul Before the Dawn of the Michael Age	19
3. The Way of Michael and What Preceded It	29
4. Michael's Task in the Sphere of Ahriman	37
5. The Experiences of Michael in the Course of His Cosmic Mission	45
6. The Activity of Michael and the Future of Humanity	53
7. The Michael-Christ Experience of Humanity	61
8. Michael's Mission in the Cosmic Age of Human Freedom	67
9. World-thoughts in the Working of Michael and in the Working of Ahriman	73
10. At the Gates of the Consciousness Soul	79
11. How the Michael-forces Work in the Earliest Unfolding of the Consciousness Soul	85
12. Hindrances and Helps to the Michael-forces	91
13. Michael's Suffering Over Human Evolution Before the Time of His Earthly Activity	97
14. A Christmas Contemplation: The Mystery of the Logos	105
References	111
Index	113

Foreword

Charles Kovacs taught at the Edinburgh Steiner School for many years. He always kept day-by-day notes of his lessons in the hope that they would be of some assistance to his fellow teachers, and several volumes of these notes have already been published by Floris with this in mind.

During his time as a teacher he was frequently called on to give lectures, and he also conducted regular evening study groups on different subjects relating to spiritual science. The present volume contains the notes of a series of study groups which he held on the subject of the mission of the Archangel Michael as described by Rudolf Steiner. These gatherings were attended by teachers, parents and a variety of interested people from Edinburgh and its surroundings.

Although Kovacs made notes beforehand, he never referred to them during the actual meetings, always speaking freely and then afterwards discussing questions asked by those present. Kovacs always read widely, and from a young age he made a special study of the work of Rudolf Steiner. This can be seen clearly in the contents of this book, which though it touches many subjects deeply is also accessible to any interested reader. Kovacs was also a fine artist and some of his works are included here, though they were not painted originally to accompany any text.

Some readers may be aware that a similar volume was published in German in 2011 by Perseus Verlag entitled *Die Sendung Michaels*. The two books have similarities but also differ in many ways. Neither book is a translation; each was given originally in its own language to different groups of people.

Howard Copland
December 2020

1

At the Dawn of the Michael Age

August 17, 1924

In January 1924 Rudolf Steiner began publishing in the weekly periodical *Das Goetheanum* regular articles or letters addressed to the members of the Anthroposophical Society. They were the outcome of the Christmas Conference held in December 1923 and were intended to establish a living communication between the Vorstand (the Executive Branch of the Society in Dornach) and the members all over the world. In some of these letters Steiner spoke to the members about what he hoped for and expected from them, but these letters were soon accompanied with the so-called *Leitsätze* – the basic principles or 'leading thoughts'. These consisted of three short paragraphs which, as they followed week after week, grew into a concise summary of anthroposophy. In all these communications there was as yet no mention of the Archangel Michael.

It was only in August, with Michaelmas approaching, that Rudolf Steiner published the first of what then came to be known as the Michael Letters. A second letter appeared at the end of the month. This was followed by a pause, but from October onwards – by which time Rudolf Steiner was already stricken by his fatal illness and bedridden – the Michael Letters continued in an unbroken sequence until Christmas 1924. There are no more Michael Letters beyond that date. The leading thoughts continued into early 1925 and came to an end with Rudolf Steiner's death.

If one reflects on the timing of these letters, appearing as they do during that part of the year most closely associated with Michael, it is easy to imagine that they were written at the behest of Michael. They are, in any case, Rudolf Steiner's last communications about the great archangel and should therefore be approached with the utmost seriousness.

The first Michael Letter, 'At the Dawn of the Michael Age', appeared on August 17, 1924. This letter presents the reader with a picture of the development of human thinking since the nineteenth century. Without an understanding of this development it is almost impossible to understand Michael's mission in the present age. The traditional image of the archangel is not sufficient to make us realise where and how the present battle between the hosts of Michael and the powers of darkness is being fought. The battlefield is our thinking, and the challenge we face today is not so much *what* we think, but *how* we think. It is quite possible to acquire anthroposophical or spiritual concepts and yet use them in a way that is far removed from all that Michael wishes to accomplish in our time.

We learn in this first Michael Letter that in the ages preceding the ninth century, people did not experience their thoughts as something they produced within themselves. What is meant in this context by 'thoughts' does not refer to the fanciful daydreaming that many people today refer to when they use the word 'thinking'. Instead it refers to those concepts that allow us to make connections between things, true concepts that provide genuine insight, so that we can say 'this is the cause and that is the effect' or 'this is the whole and that is a part of it'. It was these true concepts – these 'thoughts' – that were experienced by the people of those earlier ages as being given by higher powers, not something they produced out of their own minds.

It is very difficult for us living today to imagine ourselves with a mind that did not think thoughts, but received them instead. It will help us to understand this mind of the past

1. AT THE DAWN OF THE MICHAEL AGE

better if we go back further than the 1000 years suggested in this letter, say 3000 years to the Babylonian civilisation. At that time human beings understood the world not in the form of concepts, but in the form of pictures that appeared to them as dream pictures appear to us. But while our dreams are often puzzling and nonsensical, the waking dreams of the Babylonians and the Chaldeans were illuminating: they explained the world to them, and in the mythologies of that time we have remnants of this ancient form of knowledge.

One of these myths is of particular interest to us. In the beginning, so this myth tells us, all was chaos, a world of conflicting forces like a storm-swept sea. But this chaos was in itself a being, a being whose very nature and essence was chaos: the great dragon Tiamat. The gods, who lived in pure spiritual realms far above the dark region of Tiamat, sent the strongest and most courageous among them down to fight the dragon. This was the god Marduk. After a terrible struggle Marduk overcame the dragon and, having slain it, divided its body into different parts. From these parts Marduk fashioned the sky and the stars, the planets and the earth. Marduk gave each star its place in the firmament and set the sun and moon and planets on their courses. There was harmony and order in the world; chaos had become cosmos. And when Marduk had done all of this, the gods sang. The cosmos is the image of this heavenly choir of the gods.

The being called Marduk in the Babylonian myth was called Michael in the Hebrew tradition.[1] And what the myth describes as Marduk-Michael's power to impose order on chaos is an image, a symbol, for the power we call *intelligence*. It is intelligence that brings order into chaos. The cosmic order established by Michael is reflected in the processes of Nature here on earth: in the growth of plants, in the changes of the seasons, in the course of human life. In all the rhythmical processes of the world there lives and works the Cosmic Intelligence of Michael.

For the ancient Babylonians this intelligence revealed

itself in pictures, or imaginations, which were received by the astral body. In the following Greco-Roman civilisation these dreamlike imaginations had faded away and it was now the etheric body that perceived the Cosmic Intelligence in the form of thoughts. When we see a physical object it would not occur to us to say that our eyes have produced the image we behold; likewise it would not have occurred to Plato or Aristotle to say that their minds had produced the ideas they expressed in their philosophies. Ideas, concepts and thoughts were 'seen' by the etheric body as we see physical objects by means of our physical senses. This is indicated by the word 'idea' itself, which is derived from the Greek verb *idein*, meaning 'to see'.

The etheric body is not as isolated from the surrounding world as is the physical body. The outer etheric forces and the inner forces of the human etheric body are in continuous communication. This is why the whole of Greek philosophy never made the distinction between subject and object, between subjective viewpoints and objective facts – as is natural to us today. In the etheric world there are no sharp boundaries between inner and outer forces. An interesting example of this are the philosophies connected with the four classical elements of earth, water, air and fire. These refer not to the physical substances of earth or water, but to etheric forces. The philosopher Thales (*c*. 624–545 BC), who had a phlegmatic temperament, declared that all things had their origin in water – the watery element being associated with that particular temperament. For the same reason, the philosopher Heraclitus (*c*. 535–475 BC), a choleric, made a similar claim for fire. The philosopher Empedocles (*c*. 494–434 BC), however, saw all things as arising from the sympathy and antipathy at work between the four elements. He became so entranced by the interplay of these forces that he threw himself into the crater of Mount Etna in order to become one with this interweaving of forces.

Yet – and this too is characteristic of that age – none of these philosophers would have considered their conception of reality as a theory or a hypothesis. They 'saw' what they stated and it

1. AT THE DAWN OF THE MICHAEL AGE

was therefore not mere opinion, just as it is not for us mere opinion whether it is day or night.

From this we can more easily understand how, at a time when human minds 'saw' divine intelligence working in all there is, the question of human freedom could not arise. Human destiny was seen as a part of the intelligent world order; there could be no freedom.

The distinction between subject and object could not and did not arise as long as thought was experienced in the etheric body. The first people to make this distinction were the scholastic philosophers of the early Middle Ages: the great thinkers of the ninth, tenth, eleventh and twelfth centuries. They were all members of various monastic orders for the simple reason that only within the Church was the level of education high enough to allow for the development of intelligent thought. Among the uneducated masses, remnants of the older forms of perceiving the world, including even the dream-like imaginations of the Babylonian epoch, still persisted and would continue do so for many centuries. It is to this persistence of the old ways of seeing that we owe the fairy tales, sagas, legends and fables bequeathed to us by the Middle Ages. But among the monks whose education allowed them to develop philosophic thought, there appeared signs that a new age was coming, one in which intelligence had come down to the level of the physical body. The use of the concepts 'subject' and 'object' was one of these signs.

Among the scholastic philosophers of this time the question arises as to whether the ideas formed in our minds are subjective or objective. In the physical world there are only concrete objects. Words like 'man' and 'woman' (meaning all men and all women) and 'humanity' are subjective terms. They are coined to simplify discussion, but they do not refer to an all-encompassing objective reality. Or is there an objective spiritual reality behind the word 'humanity', for example, that embraces all human beings of all races, ages and sexes? One group of thinkers, the Nominalists, held that the terms we use to classify things that share common features – dog, tree, crystal, in fact all nouns – are mere words, names. We could say they are labels that we attach to objects as a way of ordering the flood of sense impressions, but this ordering is done purely for our own convenience. However, another group of thinkers, the Realists, claimed that these words or names indicated spiritual realities.

The Nominalist/Realist controversy really concerns intelligence itself. For a Babylonian or a Greek it was obvious that human intelligence could only arise in a world that was intelligible, a world fashioned by divine intelligence. Human intelligence was thus a reflection of divine intelligence. This was the view shared by the Realists, foremost amongst them Thomas Aquinas (1225–74). For Nominalists, however, human intelligence did not rise much above wordplay.

The answer to the Nominalists' argument can be found in a legend of ancient Jewish lore. According to this legend, the angels came before God with the complaint that he showed more favour to the newly created Adam than to all the other hierarchies. God took the angels to the paradise where Adam still lived among the plants and animals that had been placed under his dominion. God showed the animals and plants to the angels and asked them to tell him what they were. The angels did not know, but Adam called all creatures by their names. Finally, the angels understood the human being's unique position in the world that God had created.

But the legend has a much deeper meaning than may at first appear. Why should God, who created the lion and the eagle, need Adam to tell him which was the lion and which the eagle? For the same reason that we need a mirror if we want to see ourselves, even though we would exist whether there are mirrors or not. Similarly, the divine wisdom that created the world would exist whether there are human beings or not, but it cannot become conscious of itself unless and until it is reflected in human intelligence. In humanity and through humanity the divine intelligence becomes conscious of itself.

1. AT THE DAWN OF THE MICHAEL AGE

It is also important that it is Adam, meaning humanity as a whole, who names the creatures; it is not any specific individuality that reflects the light of the divine intelligence but something in the individual that is universally human. True knowledge is universal in nature: Pythagoras' Theorem is not only true for Pythagoras; likewise the evolution of humanity as described in the book *An Outline of Esoteric Science* is not only true for Rudolf Steiner. Such insights are for all of humanity, and the individuality who was the first to gain this knowledge acts only on behalf of all. If we as individuals are able to understand these insights and share them with the people who brought them, what is it that enables us to grasp these truths? It is the 'universal human' in each of us. For the Nominalists, as we have seen, the words 'man', 'woman' or 'humanity' are just abstract names that do not refer to anything real. But humankind is a reality that manifests itself every time we comprehend a universal truth, and it is also this universal human within our own individuality who recognises and responds to the universal truth of anthroposophy.

All this can lead us to a better understanding of the nature of the Archangel Michael. As distinct from angels, who are concerned with the lives of individual human beings, archangels are group spirits: they guide and inspire whole groups of human beings, such as the different nationalities on earth. But there are groups of human beings who are bound together by forces other than those of nationhood, and these non-national groups are also led by archangels. There is, for instance, an archangel who is concerned with the stream of esoteric Christianity just as there is also one for the exoteric stream of Christianity represented by the Roman Catholic Church. Michael, being an archangel, is therefore the guiding spirit of a particular group of human beings and, as it is not a national group, its members can be spread out over the whole globe.

What kind of people are the members of this group, and what is it that they all have in common?

It was mentioned before that there is present in each individual the universal human, a soul-element that is purely human and distinct from all that makes us specifically individual. In many people this universally human part of the soul remains unconscious and comes to the surface only on the occasions when the soul is stirred by compassion for other human beings. But there are also individuals in whom this universal element is present in full waking consciousness. It makes its presence felt by an interest in questions that are universally human: questions about what human beings really are, where we come from and where we go to, and what is the meaning of our existence. Souls in whom questions of this kind burn with a bright intensity belong to the group whose leader is the Archangel Michael. From this we can realise the significance of a key sentence in the very first of the leading thoughts:

> Hence only they can be anthroposophists who feel certain questions on the nature of humanity and the universe as an elemental need of life, just as one feels hunger and thirst.[2]

It is a statement that characterises those souls who belong to the Michael-stream. It is understandable that souls in whom these questions live strongly will be drawn to the Cosmic Intelligence of Michael in the form that it has assumed in our time: anthroposophy.

Like other archangels Michael becomes, for a period of about 300 years, a Time Spirit: he puts his stamp, as it were, on the epochs ruled by him. In such an epoch the universal human element appears as an increasing move toward cosmopolitanism and the urge to transcend nationality. It was so in a previous Michael Age, during the time of Alexander the Great (356–326 BC), and it is so again in our time, when technology and world trade have made the world one global village, despite the nationalistic impulses that resist this development.

1. AT THE DAWN OF THE MICHAEL AGE

In the 300-year period that began in the nineteenth century, Michael is both the group spirit of the souls to whom the universal human questions are vitally important, and the ruling Time Spirit. This is why anthroposophists must be in tune with the times and not seek refuge in spiritual practices that hark back to an earlier age. The questions that the souls belonging to Michael's group are asking cannot be answered by simple faith, they can only be answered by intelligence: the Cosmic Intelligence of Michael.

This Cosmic Intelligence is not the cold, hard cleverness that is usually evoked when the word intelligence is used. The Cosmic Intelligence of Michael is imbued with the kind of warmth and enthusiasm that artists bring to the creation of a masterpiece. It is filled with the kind of love a craftsman feels for their craft. Unless we can infuse our intelligence with this warmth we do not present to the hierarchies a true mirror-image of the Cosmic Intelligence, but a distortion. We have to think not only with our heads but also with our hearts in order to offer to the gods a true reflection of the Cosmic Intelligence. And when there is, even in the smallest way, a true reflection, then human beings become not just mirrors but vessels for the living reality of the Michael-impulse. The dragon in the macrocosm was overcome by Michael in primordial times. The dragon in the microcosm, in human beings, will only be overcome if human intelligence is united with the Cosmic Intelligence of Michael.

2

The Condition of the Human Soul Before the Dawn of the Michael Age

August 31, 1924

The first Michael Letter sets out the facts of the evolution of human thinking. It describes the change from the thinking of the Greek philosophers, who still perceived their ideas, to the thinking of the early Middle Ages, when people began to feel that they themselves produced these ideas. The second Michael Letter explores the meaning of this change.

It may at first appear that the change resulted in a loss. The Greeks experienced their ideas as endowed with life: a concept was not a mere abstraction, but a living entity. To us, concepts are as lifeless and insubstantial as shadows; any sense-impression is more real to us than the thoughts we form about it. This is the reason for the rise of a materialistic science.

What was it that imbued the world of concepts with life and reality for the Greeks? At that time ideas and concepts were still in the realm of Michael. Out of that higher realm, ideas shone into human souls. Just as we know that the light of day comes from the sun, so the Greeks knew that the light of thinking came from a sun-like source which we call Michael.

Rudolf Steiner calls Michael the *Verwalter* of the world of ideas. It means someone entrusted with the stewardship of something, a trustee or manager. The word implies that the world of ideas comes from higher spheres than Michael's, but that he is entrusted with the responsibility of sending the light of ideas, in the right measure and at the right time, into human souls. Michael is the cosmic steward of this thought-world, and as a steward he is responsible to higher beings – the gods.

From the ninth century onward this thought-world fell away from Michael and the sphere in which he holds sway and entered the human soul. Ideas and concepts do not now shine into the soul from outside or above as it were, but are at one with the soul itself. This is why we feel ourselves to be the creators of our concepts.

This is the spiritual background to the change that began in the ninth century, a change, moreover, that has enhanced rather than diminished humanity's being. Human beings could not have known real freedom unless and until concepts – in particular moral concepts – were no longer given from on high but arose in the soul itself as the soul's own creation. Something infinitely precious that once had been entrusted to Michael has been entrusted to us, to each individual human soul. Each one of us has become a steward of this precious thing called thinking, and as stewards we are responsible for the way in which we use it.

In the New Testament there is the Parable of the Talents, a 'talent' being the Roman word for a large amount of money. A rich man who has to go on a journey gives some talents to each of his three stewards to put to good use on his behalf. On his return, the rich man learns that two of the stewards have done profitable business and can hand him back twice as much as they received. They earn the rich man's praise. The third steward, however, buried his money in the earth and so can only return what he was given. He is condemned by the rich man.[1] We can see the parable as referring to the 'talent'

2. THE HUMAN SOUL BEFORE THE MICHAEL AGE

of thinking – in other words, to our intelligence and to our responsibility for making the right use of it. The steward who buried his talent in the earth represents those that use their intelligence only for earthly, material matters. From them, as it says in the parable, their 'talent' will be taken away. In our daily lives, we accept that we are responsible for our deeds, but we are not so used to regarding ourselves as responsible for the concepts and ideas that we form in our minds. Nevertheless, there is such a responsibility.

Our actions are a matter of our own individual karma and we must bear the consequences of these actions as individuals. However, as was discussed in connection with the previous letter, as thinkers it is the universal human that thinks in us. What we think and how we think – whether crude concepts or subtle ones, trivial thoughts or profound ones – affect the karma of humanity *as a whole*. When we think, we make use of that which is universally human and in turn it affects that which is universally human: humanity itself. With our deeds we build our individual karma; with our thoughts we build the karma of humanity. This is why the steward who buried his talent in the ground had this talent – the intelligence – taken away from him: he had not contributed anything to the future stages of human evolution.

As a flower grows, it first unfolds leaves and eventually the blossom. Within the blossom there are the little seeds. They look quite insignificant in comparison with the blossom, yet it is from them that future flowers will grow. The world we see around us is the blossom that has grown from the thoughts of the gods, and the worlds of the future will grow from the seemingly insignificant seeds of human thought, from our concepts and ideas. Our thoughts may seem unreal compared with the world around us, but this is only because their reality lies in the future. The future stages of world evolution are entrusted to our stewardship in the concepts we form. This is the talent for which we have to account.

When this talent descended from the realm of Michael into

human souls, the process resulted, inevitably, in a separation between humanity and the spiritual world. Human beings could now only develop and apply concepts in relation to the world they were aware of – the world of the senses. The rise of a materialistic science was therefore inevitable; it is a stage through which humanity has to pass. But while going through this stage, human intelligence, human thinking, will grow in strength and in fact became more spiritual. It is one of the paradoxes of evolution that, for some centuries now, humanity has used a very spiritual faculty to develop a completely materialistic view of the world. We have, quite literally, buried our talent in the earth.

What is Michael's part in this development? Just as each human being has a guardian angel who watches over them, so too the world of concepts and ideas has its own guardian angel, the Archangel Michael. It is Michael who watches over this thought-world on the path that leads from the past into the future, from the thoughts of the gods to the thoughts of human beings, which are the seeds of the future. And what Michael recognised as a necessity was to make human thinking, which was totally directed to the world of matter, aware of its own spiritual nature. This was undertaken in Rudolf Steiner's book *The Philosophy of Freedom*, and we must see the book in this context to realise the Michaelic impulse in it.

The next step, as necessary as the first, was to set beside the science of Nature a science of the spirit. In such a science, the thoughts and ideas already present in human souls could be used to comprehend the world of the spirit; no longer would they be directed solely towards the world of matter. It is something quite new in world evolution that ordinary human beings are credited with the ability, the talent, to comprehend the mysteries of the spirit. We would not have this ability if there had not been the descent of the Cosmic Intelligence as mentioned before. But this intelligence has come down into human souls, which is why Rudolf Steiner could say that all one needs to understand anthroposophy is ordinary common

2. THE HUMAN SOUL BEFORE THE MICHAEL AGE

sense.[2] He did add, however, that this common sense has to make a great effort to achieve real comprehension. One can read Steiner's books without such efforts, but then intelligence remains 'buried in the earth' as it were.

Students of Rudolf Steiner's work often say that they could understand his descriptions of spiritual facts better if they could 'see' what he had seen. But this is a mistaken view. At a certain time after death all human souls, including even materialists, atheists and agnostics, see the divine hierarchies, but what they see remains incomprehensible unless they have the concepts and ideas necessary for understanding. These concepts and ideas can only be acquired here on earth. Without such concepts the soul in the spiritual world is in the same situation a member of a primitive tribe would be if they were plucked from the jungle and deposited in a modern city. They would see all that is going on, but would make little sense of it.

Spiritual science would be of no value to humanity if its truth depended on clairvoyant visions. Our souls have had such visions in past incarnations. What is required in the present age is that we use the precious gift that humanity has received – concepts and ideas – to understand spiritual facts. And in as far as we are able to understand these with the same clarity as a chemist knows the chemical composition of water, so we can take this understanding with us into the life after death. There the thoughts of our earthly life become the spiritual light by means of which we comprehend what we see and experience. This too is an important aspect of the mission of Michael: that the light of concepts and ideas, which went from the spiritual world when it entered human souls on earth, is brought back to the spiritual world by these souls.

Spiritual science necessarily makes strenuous demands on our thinking when we attempt to understand it. Why is this necessary? We have seen that through the change that took place from the ninth century onward, human beings felt themselves to be the producers of their thoughts. But what is the 'self' that produces these concepts and ideas, if it is not the separate, personal self that also feels hunger and experiences anger? The self that is engaged in thinking and forming concepts is nothing less than what we have previously called the universal human in us. It is the Spirit Self or Manas.

Because our concepts to begin with are so shadowy, so lacking in substance and reality, the self that thinks them appears even less substantial, even less real. Yet this is the self we should become conscious of in the present epoch of the consciousness soul, and the only way to make us more conscious of this higher self is to make the task of thinking and forming concepts harder. We only become aware of certain muscles if we exercise them, and the harder we make them work the more conscious we are of them. Similarly, it is only by wrestling with our thinking that we can awaken to the reality of our higher self.

There was an occasion in the distant past when a certain individual had to undergo an experience that bears a resemblance to our modern task. At the time this task fell to one man, not humanity as a whole, and what he did has to be understood as a necessary preparation for the Mystery of Golgotha. This man is the patriarch Jacob. In Genesis 32:22–30 it is written that Jacob, having sent his family away, was alone by the Jabbok ford. During that night he wrestled with a stranger. When dawn came the stranger tried to break free, but Jacob would not let him go until the stranger had blessed him. The blessing was given and Jacob called the place where this had happened Peniel.

At the time of Jacob, thinking worked as an instinctive force in the darkness of the unconscious. This instinctive thinking is what we now call cunning. Jacob in the Old Testament, as well as the Greek hero Odysseus, are shown in their respective sagas as possessing great cunning. It is the early, primitive, instinctive form of thinking. We may be repelled by the tricks played by Jacob or Odysseus, but both were initiates who had developed the forces of thought in the form that was possible at that time. However, it falls to Jacob to take thinking further, to raise it from the darkness of the instinctual life into the daylight of consciousness. This is the purpose of his struggle.

The stranger with whom Jacob wrestles is the Archangel Michael, the steward of the thought-world, who worked at that time as the servant of Yahweh in the unconscious part of the soul. Michael gives his blessing to Jacob so that from then onward not mere cunning but wise, conscious thinking – *wisdom* – will flow into the generations that descend from Jacob. This 'wisdom-stream' is later represented by King Solomon, who in turn is the ancestor of the Solomonic Jesus child, the reincarnation of the Persian prophet Zarathustra. This is what was prepared in that night of Jacob's wrestling. And the name that Jacob gave to the place where it occurred, Peniel, means the 'countenance of God', which is Michael's esoteric name.

It is of the utmost importance for an understanding of the being that Jacob wrestles with, that he is called the 'countenance of God' (more precisely, the name Michael translates as 'Who is like God'). When Rudolf Steiner gave the Christian Community a special Michaelmas prayer, he did not use the word Michael at all, not once. Instead, the priest calls on the community to behold with their souls' eyes 'the countenance of him who is himself the countenance of the God of humankind'.[3] In this solemn moment of the service not the traditional but the esoteric name of the archangel is used.

What does the 'countenance of God' mean? At all times and in all regions human beings have always recognised the people they know by their faces. Even the use of passport photos demonstrates that the recognition of someone's identity is connected with the face. We recognise each other by our faces. How do we recognise the God in us? How do we recognise that which is of a divine-spiritual nature in us? There must be something in us which reveals our spiritual nature as unmistakably as a face reveals a friend.

In one of his fundamental works, *Theosophy*, Rudolf Steiner makes it clear from the start what it is that reveals a human being's spiritual nature. In order to introduce the trinity of body, soul and spirit, he takes as his starting point an everyday experience. I see a flower, which is made possible by the sense organs of the physical body. I enjoy the colour or scent of the flower, which is an experience of the soul. I recognise that the flower is of a particular kind, say a rose. I have the concept or idea of 'rose', which is the permanent principle behind all transient, perishable roses. This conception is an act of the spirit. I am a spiritual being because I can form the concept 'rose' – in other words, because I can think. It is in thinking, in the forming of concepts and ideas, that the human being's divine nature reveals itself and can be recognised. Thinking is thus the 'countenance of God' in the human being. This is the reason why Michael – the cosmic steward of the thought-world who inspires us with thought – is called the countenance of God: Peniel.

The task of Jacob was to raise thinking from the instinctive level of cunning to the conscious level of objective reflection where it can become wisdom. And because at that time Yahweh, the God of the hereditary forces, was still preparing the coming of Christ, the ability that Jacob had wrestled from Michael was passed on through the generations until the birth of the Zarathustra or Solomonic Jesus child, as described in the Gospel of Matthew.

In our time once again thinking has to be raised to a still higher level where humanity can begin to develop the forces of Manas, or Spirit Self. But this time every individual must perform the task for themselves, the ability cannot be passed on through the blood. Michael can no longer be found in the darkness of the unconscious but in the broad daylight of the fully awakened mind. We no longer have to wrestle with him either, but instead with the powers of darkness that want to persuade us that it is all too difficult, that we are not clever enough, that there are more pressing matters to think about than anthroposophical problems, and that we should bury our talent deep in the earth.

3

The Way of Michael and What Preceded It

October 12, 1924

After August 31, there is no reference to Michael for several weeks. But on October 12, the Michael theme is taken up again and remains the main content of the letters until Christmas. In this third letter Rudolf Steiner describes the four stages, or steps, that brought thinking to the shadow-like form it has in the present age. In the first stage, in very ancient times, thoughts were experienced in the 'I' as living spiritual *beings*. In the second stage, thoughts were experienced in the astral body, this time as the *revelation* of spiritual beings. In the third stage, the etheric body experienced thoughts as *living forces*. It is only in the present age, from the fifteenth century onwards, that human beings know thought as a shadow, experienced in the physical body.

We can see from these stages that as long as thoughts were experienced as realities, the 'I' could not awaken to its own reality. It was only when thoughts had been reduced to lifeless shadows that I-consciousness could arise. At this stage thoughts, concepts and ideas were no longer recognised in their true inner nature, which is spiritual, but were used to comprehend the sense world. This is the origin of modern science.

In this Michael Letter the whole process is described

in just a few sentences, but Rudolf Steiner gave a very detailed description of this process in his book *The Riddles of Philosophy*. Even among anthroposophists, this is not a work widely read, which is a pity, especially if one considers what Rudolf Steiner revealed about this book in a lecture he gave on January 10, 1915.[1] In this lecture Steiner spoke of beings who, during the present Earth evolution, go through stages of evolution that repeat the ancient Saturn, ancient Sun and ancient Moon evolutions. What is of special interest in the context of this third Michael Letter is the description of beings who use this Earth evolution to accomplish their own Sun evolution. But even more interesting and surprising is the remark Steiner made about these beings: he said he had once written a biography of such a being, his book *The Riddles of Philosophy*.

This seemingly abstract pattern of the descent of thought, from the inward experience of the 'I' to the outer sheaths of humanity, in fact constitutes the life story of a spiritual being who has here on earth a Sun-nature. And the name by which we know this Sun being is 'Philosophy'.

We human beings speculate. We form ideas about this or that, we 'philosophise' with every generalisation we utter and with every judgment we pass. But in all these thoughts entities of a much higher nature than ours have their life and being: in particular, the Sun being whose earthly name is Philosophy – the love of wisdom. What does it mean that this being is now going through its Sun evolution? On ancient Sun it was the turn of the archangels to go through the stage at which humanity is today. And the being known as Philosophy is at present an archangel at the human stage. Would not the discipline of philosophy therefore serve a wonderful purpose as a link between humans and archangels?

It must be so, for on the day when he spoke to members for the last time, on September 28, 1924, the evening before Michaelmas, Rudolf Steiner ended his lecture with a mantric verse that begins with these words:

3. THE WAY OF MICHAEL AND WHAT PRECEDED IT

> You beings, descended from the Sun Powers,
> Radiant, grace-bestowing Spirits of might,
> Divine thought has pre-ordained
> Your becoming Michael's shining raiment.[2]

It is the being, Philosophy, which is preordained to become the raiment of Michael. But then, of course, Philosophy will be something very different from what it was, and very different from the picture people have in their minds when they use the word. The lifeless abstractions taught in our universities as philosophy have to be brought to life, have to become 'radiant, grace-bestowing'. And what does philosophy become when it shines as Michael's raiment? Anthroposophy.

But this life story of philosophy, its path from thoughts experienced as living spiritual realities to lifeless abstractions, and then the quickening of these dead thoughts to new life, can also be told in a different form. When thoughts were experienced in the 'I' as realities, human beings knew themselves through the thoughts that connected them with the spiritual world, which is their true home, or their true mother. As thought began its descent, falling away from the spiritual world, human beings felt as if they had lost their true mother, and as the world of the senses appeared more real, they felt themselves as though given over to a 'stepmother'. The motif in fairy tales of the evil stepmother has nothing to do with real stepmothers, but with the Ahrimanic forces of the sense world, which is the 'stepmother' of the human spirit. It is Ahriman, working from the sense world, who tries to destroy the life in human thought.

It is Ahriman's onslaught on human thought that is described imaginatively in the story of Snow White. In the story the evil stepmother has a magic mirror of which she asks who the most beautiful woman in the land is, hoping that it is her. Of course, if there were no higher worlds, the sense world would be the most beautiful of all worlds. But as long as there was still any life in human thought, human beings knew, through the nature of thought itself, that there were higher, more beautiful worlds than this one. Snow White is the thought-life that conveys the beauty of these worlds, and the magic mirror that answers the evil queen is human consciousness.

For a time, in Greece and even later in parts of Europe, thought was experienced in the etheric body. In their souls human beings felt connected through thought with etheric forces, with the elementary beings of the etheric world. These are the Seven Dwarfs of the fairy tale, for there are seven kinds of etheric forces. But this last connection with supersensible worlds had to come to an end. Thinking descended to the physical body, to the level of the mineral world where Ahriman holds sway and where Ahrimanic forces render thinking lifeless. This is portrayed in the fairy tale by the stepmother tricking Snow White into eating a poisoned apple. The apple is the symbol of the sense world. In the Old Testament it is Lucifer who induces Adam and Eve to eat the apple. They become more deeply immersed in the sense world than Yahweh had intended for them. But with this 'fall' there also begins humanity's road to freedom. In the story of Snow White, it is Ahriman who completes the task of making human beings free: through his influence thinking becomes lifeless, and lifeless thoughts are used to explain the sense world. Again the symbol of the apple represents involvement with the world of the senses.

The picture we form about ourselves and the world, the philosophy that underlies the scientific view of the world that has developed since the fifteenth century, this is the glass coffin in which Snow White is placed. The philosophic systems presented in Steiner's *The Riddles of Philosophy* are just so many coffins each containing a lifeless Snow White. Now when the evil stepmother looks into the mirror of human consciousness she hears what she wants to hear: that she is the most beautiful woman in the land, meaning the material world is the most beautiful because for human consciousness no other world exists.

3. THE WAY OF MICHAEL AND WHAT PRECEDED IT

Not just scientists and philosophers, but all who live in this age have a thinking symbolised by lifeless Snow White. What does the name Snow White mean? In a lecture on colour Rudolf Steiner calls white 'the image of the spirit',[3] and a snowflake is a tiny crystal, the dead image of the spirit. Yet there is also something else implied by the name Snow White: purity. This is, indeed, what has been gained by the descent of thought into the realm of death: a purification or, to use the Greek word, a *catharsis*. Just as Lucifer was necessary to make human beings capable of choosing freely between good and evil, so Ahriman was necessary to purge our thinking of personal likes and dislikes, from subjective bias, and make it truly objective.

In ancient Greece, the philosopher Thales regarded water as the origin of all things, an idea rooted in his own phlegmatic temperament. With Heraclitus it was his choleric temperament that induced him to place fire at the beginning. But in the scientific thinking of the present age there is no room for such purely personal judgments. In this respect human thinking has become Snow White. Only a thinking that has become free of all personal elements, which has become impersonal, can be universally human, capable of expressing truths that are valid for humanity as a whole. But this lifeless thinking must at some point be brought back to life. In the fairy tale, Snow White is revived by a prince. Who is this prince?

To understand this symbolic figure, we have to turn again to the four stages of the descent of thinking as outlined in this Michael Letter. In the first stage, when thoughts were experienced as living realities in the 'I', the one thought that could not be experienced was the thought of the 'I' itself. There could be no I-consciousness. It is only in the last stage, when thoughts have become lifeless shadows produced by the 'I' that I-consciousness could arise. It is just when the 'I' feels itself to be the thinker of thoughts that there is an I-consciousness. But what is this 'I' that thinks?

There is something in us that is concerned with questions

that are universally human, existential questions that are far removed from those arising out of our own personal circumstances. This something is the universal human being in each one of us. If we replace the word 'human' by its Greek equivalent 'Anthropos', then we can say that it is the Anthropos in each one of us who is asking these questions about the meaning and purpose of human existence. I-consciousness, in the sense in which Rudolf Steiner uses the term, does not refer to our ordinary self-awareness, but to an awareness of the Anthropos in us.

It is the Anthropos in us who can recognise in the dead thoughts – in Snow White – that they are 'dead images of the Spirit'. It is the Anthropos in us who can free thoughts and ideas from sense impressions and achieve sense-free thinking. It is the Anthropos in us who can awaken the dead thoughts to new life. This is the prince who rescues Snow White from her death-like sleep.

According to Steiner, a modern interpretation of the word Anthropos would be 'one who looks up into the heights'.[4] It is only by seeking our true being in spiritual heights that we manifest our human nature, our humanity. This 'looking upwards' is, and always was, accomplished through thinking: once this was done in the form of images, now it is done in the form of concepts and ideas. And if we direct our thinking towards the heights of the spiritual world, there comes to meet us the being whose shining raiment these thoughts are: Michael.

At the end of this Michael Letter Rudolf Steiner writes: 'It is Michael's mission to bring into human etheric bodies the forces through which the thought-shadows may regain *life*.'[5] This means that thinking, which has descended to the physical body and has become a shadow of itself, has to be raised to the etheric body, and the forces needed to achieve this come from Michael. What kind of forces are these?

They are the forces of the light-ether. The same forces which manifest themselves in the world outside as light exist within us in the form of thought or, one could say, as 'inner

3. THE WAY OF MICHAEL AND WHAT PRECEDED IT

light'. We can understand the nature of these forces if we observe how they work in Nature, for instance in the development of a caterpillar. At a certain stage a caterpillar spins its cocoon. As Rudolf Steiner explained in a lecture to the workmen, in making the cocoon the caterpillar spins his whole physical body into the rays of the sun.[6] The silkworm dies into the sun's rays and there remains only the lifeless shell of the cocoon. But inside the cocoon the 'inner light' creates something new and quite different from the earth-bound caterpillar.

As the butterfly arises from the dead chrysalis, so the living thought arises from the dead thought-shadows, from the abstract ideas and concepts of modern human beings. And what brings about both transformations are the Sun-forces of the light-ether given to us by the Archangel of the Sun, Michael.

4

Michael's Task in the Sphere of Ahriman

October 19, 1924

The aim of the fourth Michael Letter is to make us aware of the task that confronts us in the current epoch of the consciousness soul. In the age of the sentient soul, when the Egyptian and Babylonian civilisations flourished, the human 'I' worked unconsciously on the astral body. In the following Greco-Roman period, during the age of the intellectual soul, the work of the 'I' was directed towards the etheric body. In both of these stages human beings were not left on their own; they were helped and supported by higher beings. Since the fifteenth century, when the development of the consciousness soul began, the 'I' has had to descend into the realm of the forces of the physical body. The higher beings who accompanied humanity in previous stages do not enter this realm. It is the realm of death; and Ahriman, whom human beings encounter, is the Lord of Death.

There is an image that appears around this time which can be regarded as the perfect expression of the change taking place at the transition from the Greco-Roman epoch to the present one. From about the fourteenth century onwards there appears in art a theme that had not existed before: the pietà, the image of the Mother Mary with the body of Christ in her lap following his crucifixion. There is no passage in the Gospels to account for the appearance of this theme in painting and sculpture, nor was there any tradition that could have given rise to it. The pietà appeared because the people of that time recognised, in their feelings rather than in clear thoughts, that this image represented something in their souls: the encounter with death. We have been familiar with the death of the physical body ever since the Fall, but our inner soul-forces had not been touched by the death process. It was only now, toward the end of the Middle Ages, that the soul felt death entering its own being in the form of dead thoughts. The intellect and its abstract concepts constitute the 'corpse' that has existed in the human soul since the fourteenth century. But the symbol of the pietà means more than this. It is the dead body of Christ that lies in his mother's lap that symbolises the promise of resurrection. The power that overcame death through the Mystery of Golgotha, is also the force that raises dead thoughts to new life. The death of thought and the message that these thoughts will live again: this was what the image of the pietà conveyed to the hearts of people at the beginning of the consciousness soul epoch.

An especially beautiful representation of the pietà is Michelangelo's sculpture in St Peter's Church in Rome. Rudolf Steiner speaks of this masterpiece in the lecture series *Christ and the Spiritual World*.[1] He draws attention to the youthful looks of the mother and points out that she could be a bride mourning her dead bridegroom. He goes on to say that this is how the pietà theme is presented in Wolfram von Eschenbach's story of Parsifal. In the course of his wanderings in search of the Grail, Parsifal comes three times upon his cousin, Sigune, holding the body of her dead bridegroom, Schionatulander. The image of the woman with the corpse of the man she loves is an essential feature of the Grail legend.

There is still a third occasion when this image occurs in an esoteric context: in Goethe's *Fairy Tale of the Green Snake and the Beautiful Lily*. In this fairy tale it is the beautiful Lily who holds

4. MICHAEL'S TASK IN THE SPHERE OF AHRIMAN

in her arms the body of a young man. This too is a pietà image, and it marks the crisis point of the story. From that moment on, all subsequent events are directed towards restoring the young man to life. What matters to us in the context of the Michael Letters is the spiritual source of this fairy tale. Rudolf Steiner spoke of a Michael School that existed in the spiritual world in the nineteenth century at the time Goethe wrote his fairy tale, and the inspiration for the story came from this school. Michael is the source of the fairy tale and of the images presented in it.[2]

There was another Michael School, about 400 years earlier, at the beginning of the consciousness soul epoch. There can be no doubt that it was this school, and that it was also Michael, who gave the impulse to the pietà images of that time. When we understand that it is Michael who has the task of infusing dead thoughts with new life, then we can recognise that the image of the pietà appeared as a result of his impulse. It is Michael who speaks to us through these images.

At the time of this earlier Michael School there also existed another school. Another being had gathered together his followers to prepare his onslaught against the coming development of the consciousness soul. This being was Ahriman, and what he inspired from the dark caverns of his realm was the invention of the printing press.[3] Books, cheaply produced and in great numbers, now came into the world. Words fixed on the page that lent themselves to rigid interpretation made them the right vehicle for spreading the dead thoughts of the new age. The next development was the broadsheet, which became the newspaper, and with this was born the power of the press to form and influence people's thoughts. Radio and television eventually followed and that power increased. Instead of human beings producing their own thoughts, which is to be the great achievement of the present epoch, the media are doing this thinking for them. This is Ahriman's great counterstroke. Humanity has to choose between these powerful Ahrimanic influences and the impulse that originated in the second

Michael School at the beginning of the nineteenth century. The souls who took part in that school have been incarnating since the middle of the nineteenth century: they are the souls who were drawn to Rudolf Steiner's anthroposophy. It is their task to carry the teaching of the Michael School into the stream of human evolution.

What was the teaching they received before they entered earthly existence? It was anthroposophy, but not in the form in which it is given here on earth. Michael's instruction took the form of mighty imaginations, and Goethe's fairy tale – inspired by the Michael School – represents these cosmic imaginations in miniature. We therefore have to seek in this fairy tale an indication of what is needed to rescue thinking from the grip of Ahriman.

As we have seen, there is in the fairy tale a moment which presents a kind of pietà picture. The young man has died and his lifeless body lies in the arms of the beautiful Lily. It is the image of a thinking from which all life forces have departed. What is it that eventually restores life to the young man? It is an act of self-sacrifice performed by the enigmatic figure called the Green Snake. But what is the meaning of this symbolic creature?

No student of history could overlook a characteristic feature of the epoch which began in the fifteenth century, the epoch of the consciousness soul. In the 600 years from the beginning of this epoch to the present day, more inventions have been made than in all the preceding millennia of human existence on earth. But this inventive power was not limited to technical achievements. The great works of art, literature and music in these few centuries are creations of this same power of invention. It is a creative power – the power to imagine something before it is really here. It is unfortunate that the most suitable name for this creative force has become associated with illusion and deception, but this flawed interpretation is just another Ahrimanic device. In spite of all objections, the right name for this inventive creativity is imagination. Another

4. MICHAEL'S TASK IN THE SPHERE OF AHRIMAN

word is fantasy, derived from an old Greek verb *phaino* (φαίνω) which means to shine, to give light.

It was Goethe who spoke of an 'exact imagination', an imagination that is as precise and disciplined as mathematics. Without this kind of utterly truthful imagination it is not possible to understand his archetypal plant or his theory of colours. It was Rudolf Steiner who pointed to a still higher level of imagination. In *The Philosophy of Freedom* he introduced the concept of *moralische Phantasie*, usually translated as 'moral imagination' or 'moral fantasy'. Without this moral imagination there can be no freedom for human souls.

In Goethe's fairy tale, the power of imagination is what the Green Snake stands for. As long as this imagination is used for technical inventions it serves only our selfish and most material interests. But it is raised to a higher level in art, freed from the subjective elements of the soul through the exact imagination of Goethean science. Moral imagination bestows on human beings the freedom of selflessness, the freedom to act purely out of love for the deed itself.

This raising of imagination to ever higher levels is the sacrifice of the Green Snake. This path of the transformation of imagination is also indicated by a verse that Rudolf Steiner gave to school teachers, a verse usually spoken at the opening of the weekly meeting of teachers in Waldorf schools:

> Imbue yourself with the power of imagination,
> Have courage for the truth,
> Sharpen your feeling for responsibility of soul.[4]

The first line calls for the artistic imagination that is essential for the task of educating. The second line refers to exact, truthful imagination. The third line calls for the sense of moral responsibility that is inseparable from true freedom; it is a call for the teachers to develop moral imagination. Although this verse was given to teachers, it contains a message valid for all who regard themselves as followers of Rudolf Steiner.

There are, however, some difficulties that must be overcome if imagination is to be raised to the levels indicated by this verse. Imagination by itself is not a producer of illusion, falsehood and deceit, as the philistines of this world would have us believe. In the third Mystery Play there is Rudolf Steiner's fairy tale about the being of Imagination in which this being is sent to human beings on earth by the 'Father of Truth'. It is our selfish nature, therefore, that can falsify the true nature of imagination.

There is a certain moment in the evolution of humanity when this darkening of the light of imagination became possible. According to Steiner, in *The Riddles of Philosophy*, it was during the early stages of Greek philosophy. Up until that time imagination and logic were joined together in human thinking, not two separate faculties. This is the secret of ancient mythologies and fairy tales: they possess an inner logic infused with the power of imagination, which is why both myths and fairy tales are often truer than true. Imagination and logic were still joined together in a single faculty in early Greek philosophers, but then came the separation. Imagination became more subjective, logic more objective, and in due course, the categories of 'subject' and 'object' appeared in philosophy. Now, in the Michael Age, imagination must once again be raised to the objective standard of logic, and logic must once again be filled with the warmth and life of imagination.

The time when the split between imagination and logic occurred was also the time when the Sun Spirit, Christ, left the Sun. He has since then united himself with the earth, and it is his power which enables us to restore the unity of imagination and logic. This is the particular aspect of the Sun-Mystery revealed in this fourth Michael Letter.

Goethe's fairy tale expresses the existing duality in the symbols of the Green Snake (for imagination) and the two Will-o'-the-Wisps (for logic in philosophy and science). The Will-o'-the-Wisps scatter gold pieces all over the place. The Green Snake swallows them all and as a result begins to shine

4. MICHAEL'S TASK IN THE SPHERE OF AHRIMAN

with a golden light. The gold of the Will-o'-the-Wisps is the objective approach to all questions, which is characteristic of modern science and philosophy. Notwithstanding the materialistic outlook and the dead, abstract concepts, there is in science and philosophy, as they have developed since the fifteenth century, a striving for objective validity in their findings, and this striving is pure gold. When the Green Snake takes these gold pieces into itself, they begin to shine with a golden light, and gold is the symbol of wisdom.

But what is this fairy tale itself? It is pure imagination and at the same time expresses a profound truth that possesses a logic of its own: the logic of the evolution of thought. Goethe's fairy tale is itself an embodiment of the Green Snake shining with the golden light of wisdom. It could hardly be otherwise, being inspired by Michael. No wonder that it occupied Rudolf Steiner's mind for many years until he gave it a new form in the first Mystery Play.

The consciousness soul could not develop, and we human beings could not become free personalities, which is the aim of this development, without entering a sphere of existence where we are directly exposed to the forces of Ahriman. But only in the Ahrimanic darkness can we find the Sun forces which, since the Mystery of Golgotha, are only to be found on earth – they are spiritual gold. Michael, the Archangel of the Sun, calls us to the task of bringing this gold back to the cosmos in our thinking through the union of imagination and logic.

5

The Experiences of Michael in the Course of His Cosmic Mission

October 26, 1924

The fifth Michael Letter speaks again of the descent of the Cosmic Intelligence, but this time from the point of view of Michael himself. During the first stage divine beings are active, acting according to their own motives. Humanity meanwhile occupies only 'one corner' of this world, as Rudolf Steiner puts it. However, Michael is already concerned with humanity and safeguards our existence and future development by means of a power that is akin to intelligence. This intelligence differs from our present intelligence in that it actively participates in world processes: it expresses itself through *deeds*.

Which phase of evolution is being referred to here? It is the ancient Moon evolution, when the Dynamis, or Spirits of Movement, endowed the Moon-beings with astral forces, the forces of desire. Human beings at this point were still united with higher beings, with the Exusiai, or Spirits of Form, and so were not directly involved in the events which took place on the ancient Moon. In the lecture given on April 14, 1909 Rudolf Steiner speaks of a War in Heaven between the backward and advanced Spirits of Movement,[1] and in the lecture given on December 21, 1903 we find the following description:

> The starry heavens with its immutable laws was not always the cosmos that appears to us today. This cosmos came forth from chaos. What we have today evolved from surging waves of forces.[2]

This is the period referred to in the Michael Letter when the Spirits of Movement acted for reasons and motives of their own. But this is also the time referred to in the Babylonian myth mentioned in the discussion on the first Michael Letter: the time of Marduk-Michael's battle with the great dragon Tiamat. Michael's intelligence was not of a contemplative nature; rather it was the power that subdued the dragon and the chaos it had wrought and gave rise to the ordered universe, the cosmos. In the present Earth evolution human souls are like the cosmos during the Moon evolution, a chaotic battlefield of contending forces, but there will come a future when human souls will be as the cosmos is now, ordered and harmonious.

The German mystic Angelus Silesius (1624–77) had this distant goal in mind when he wrote the following lines:

> When you impose stillness and peace
> On inner turmoil and fight,
> Michael subdues the dragon
> And throws him down from the height.

Silesius saw in Michael's cosmic deed what human beings have to do in the microcosm of their own souls. Michael imposed order on the macrocosmic chaos, but he will not interfere with human freedom and do for us what we must do for ourselves. However, the power he used in the War in Heaven, the power of the Cosmic Intelligence, has descended to us. It has been given to us, although not as a force but only in the insubstantial, powerless form of our ideas and concepts. The force has to come from our own will. This constitutes our freedom. But the fanatic who is possessed by some idea, whose ideas have power over them, is not free, but enslaved.

5. THE EXPERIENCES OF MICHAEL

Michael upholds the order of the macrocosm but he does not want to impose this order on the microcosm, on human beings. There is, however, another being who is concerned with order and intelligence. For this being, freedom is chaos and disorder that must be eliminated and replaced by the mechanical order of which he is the great master. This being is Ahriman. He has been denied a part in creating the macrocosmic order established by Michael, and so now he wants to impose his kind of order where there is a power vacuum, so to speak, in the microcosm, in the souls of human beings.

From the twilight of the early Middle Ages, when ordinary people still thought in dream-like images but felt the approach of Ahriman's thinking, there has come down to us a fairy tale that is nothing less than a portrait of this thinking. It is the story of 'The Valiant Little Tailor'. In the previous epochs of human evolution the soul had felt the physical body to be a kind of garment. Insofar as this physical body contains dead mineral matter – for instance, the nerves and the bones – Ahriman plays a part in making this garment: he is the 'tailor'. However, with the approach of the consciousness soul epoch, Ahriman is no longer limited to this task; he aims to take possession of higher things, namely the human soul. In the fairy tale, the little tailor prepares himself a slice of bread with jam, which attracts a swarm of flies. The little tailor swats at the flies with a piece of cloth and kills seven of them. Inspired by this deed, he makes himself a belt with the inscription 'seven in one stroke'. He abandons his craft and goes out into the world to make his fortune. One of the ancient names of the Ahrimanic power is Beelzebub, which means Lord of Flies. The feat performed by the little tailor is meant to indicate his kinship with the Lord of Flies. The inscription, 'seven in one stroke', indicates that the instinctive knowledge of man's sevenfoldness will be wiped out. Through the intelligence represented by the little tailor, human beings will know themselves only as a physical body.

In the adventures that follow, the little tailor encounters a number of giants whom he outsmarts using sheer trickery.

The giants represent the forces of Nature and the tricks used by the tailor to subdue them symbolise the technological achievements of our age. From the point of view of the fairy tale, which is also the point of view of the spiritual world, our machines and gadgets are the tricks we use to subdue the forces of Nature and make them subservient to our physical comforts. One could hardly find a better image of this than the scene in which the giant carries an enormous tree whilst the little tailor, who is supposed to be carrying the other end of the tree, sits in the branches and lets the giant carry him as well. The trucks that thunder along our roads today, with their drivers sitting their cabins, is a realisation of this image.

Later in the fairy tale, in order to gain the hand of a princess, the little tailor has to perform three tasks. He must overcome two giants, tame a unicorn and capture a wild boar. To deal with the giants the little tailor sets them against each other, and in the struggle both are killed. The two giants represent the head- and limb-systems in human nature. This polarity should be reconciled and held in balance by the rhythmic-system, but the Ahrimanic intelligence is not concerned with reconciling the polarities; instead it wants to intensify the opposing tendencies. As a result, the head-system falls prey to nervous disorders and nervous breakdowns, while the will forces of the limb-system exhaust themselves in numerous ways: through work ('workaholic' is a word coined in our time), various forms of sport and intense physical activity that do nothing for real health, and in the ever increasing violence in our society.

The little tailor tames the unicorn by rousing the beast to anger and then leaping behind a tree when it charges at him. The unicorn rams its horn into the tree and cannot free itself. The little tailor cuts the horn off with an axe and now the creature is no longer dangerous. Like the horse, the unicorn is a symbol of intelligence. The true intelligence, which the gods intended for humanity, gets stuck in the dead wood of materialistic science. It becomes the prisoner of Ahrimanic intelligence.

5. THE EXPERIENCES OF MICHAEL

The little tailor deals with the wild boar by fleeing through the open door of a chapel, jumping out through a window and closing the door behind the pursuing boar. The animal is caught and can only run in circles inside the chapel. The wild boar represents man's selfish, anti-social instincts. Ahriman has no way and no intention of transforming these instincts, but he wants order and so social behaviour must be enforced. At first this was enforced by the Church, hence the chapel in the fairy tale. A traditional, received morality, based on conventions and imposed from without, works in this way. It keeps the beast imprisoned but does not transform it.

Having performed the three tasks, the tailor marries the princess. But this is not the familiar happy ending found in many other fairy tales, and one can only admire the wisdom that created this fable. The princess finds out that the hero is only a tailor and wants to get rid of him. She persuades some servants to kill him in his sleep, but the attempt fails and she has to remain married to him. The princess represents the human soul, which, beguiled by the apparent achievements of Ahrimanic intelligence, is taken over by it. When, at last, it is realised that this is not the wisdom of higher beings but of an inferior spirit, Ahriman, there arises the wish to throw off his yoke. Many of the alternative currents found in the so-called New Age spirituality of today stem from this wish, but they are doomed to failure. Ahriman is destined to remain humanity's companion until a very distant future. We cannot get rid of Ahriman and we cannot get rid of Lucifer. We can only maintain a balance between them. The clarity of Ahrimanic thinking found in materialistic science must not be lost; instead it must be raised to a higher clarity through the science of the spirit, enlivened by the exact imagination mentioned in connection with the previous Michael Letter.

As the story of the valiant little tailor shows us, Ahriman can teach us tricks to make the forces of Nature serve our material comforts, but, as humanity is belatedly finding out, Nature is making us pay a heavy price for this arrogance. Michael is not concerned with technological innovations to make life on earth easier and more comfortable. He expects us to read in the Book of Nature, for in this book, if it is read with reverence, we find the intelligence of the gods.

The intelligence we find in the kingdoms of Nature, however, is an intelligence of the past. In the present mineral kingdom we find expressed the intelligence of ancient Saturn, in the plant kingdom the intelligence of ancient Sun, and in the animal kingdom the intelligence of ancient Moon. What Nature reveals to us is the divine wisdom that was a living, active presence in previous stages of evolution. But it was not intelligence as we understand the word today. It was action, it was deed, and it was not merely wise but morally good. When some very old traditions connect certain precious stones with certain virtues, when in the Middle Ages flowers and animals were chosen as heraldic emblems, there was in all this an instinctive feeling that the forms of Nature had their origin in the moral actions of divine beings. Today we can only find the intelligence which created them in these forms, not the moral powers that were united with this intelligence in the past. Nature, in our current stage of evolution, is amoral.

Ahriman wants to absorb all the intelligence of the past, as embodied in the beings and forces of Nature, but he is only concerned with an intelligence that is bereft of moral qualities. His mighty intelligence is, from the start, amoral (just as the little tailor in the story is quite amoral) and it is this that makes him so dangerous to us at the present time. In human beings today, intelligence and morality are sharply divided. We use intelligence to gain objective knowledge of the world, whereas morality is seen as a matter of personal conviction – or the absence of such conviction. The division between subject and object, which began with the scholastic philosophers, has eventually led to the division between intelligence and morality. And our intelligence, separated from morality, makes us easy prey for Ahriman.

5. THE EXPERIENCES OF MICHAEL

To prevent a person with little moral strength but adequate intelligence from gaining access to higher knowledge, the ancient mystery schools subjected those who sought such knowledge to incredibly severe tests of their moral character. A remnant of this remains, though reduced to a mere formality, in the degree rituals of Freemasonry.

But the ancient mysteries and the principles on which they were founded have been replaced by one mystery which is open to all human souls: the Mystery of Golgotha. In Christ, wisdom and love are one, and this oneness can transform the morally neutral concepts of our intelligence so that they engender moral impulses. This morality is not imposed from outside, as it was in the ancient mysteries, but springs up from one's own being.

Michael sees the Cosmic Intelligence descending into the region where it becomes amoral and is exposed to Ahriman. But this is also the region where Christ can be found as the redeemer of this intelligence. And because Christ is present on earth, the sacred knowledge of the past, the spiritual knowledge guarded jealously in the ancient mysteries, is in the present Age of Michael given freely and openly to all who seek it, in the form of anthroposophy.

6

The Activity of Michael and the Future of Humanity

November 2, 1924

The sixth Michael Letter leads to deeper understanding of the nature of Michael. We are also given here very specific – one could say 'Michaelic' – concepts for the stages of the descent of the Cosmic Intelligence. At first human beings are united with and part of the *being* of the gods. At the second stage a separation occurs. The gods now reveal themselves by means of the stars; this is the stage of *revelation*. The third stage removes human beings still further from their origin and they see in the world around them only the *effects* of the gods, but there is still an awareness that divine beings have produced these effects. This awareness is lost in the fourth and final stage, when humanity is confronted with the finished *work* of the gods.

These four stages marking the descent of the Cosmic Intelligence, from being through revelation and effect to finished work, mirror the stages through which the soul passes when, after the 'cosmic midnight hour', it descends to its next incarnation on Earth. This downward journey begins in Devachan, the 'dwelling of the gods'. The soul then descends to the world of the stars, where it clothes itself in an astral body. At the next stage it forms its etheric body. This is a body of formative forces, and these forces are the 'effects' of the gods. Finally, the soul descends into the physical body, which it receives from its parents as the 'finished work' of the gods. There is therefore a parallel between the descent of the soul to earthly existence and the descent of Cosmic Intelligence in the course of humanity's evolution. One descent concerns us as individuals, the other concerns us as members of the human race. In each case one veil after another is added, hiding from us the divine powers that are our true origin.

In ancient Egypt – where human beings thought in images and not in abstract concepts – this was expressed in the heavily veiled statue of Isis in the city of Saïs. It bore the inscription: 'I am what was and is and will be. No mortal may lift my veils.' But the human being is not only a mortal being. As the poet Novalis wrote, it is the immortal, eternal part of us, that part of us that 'was and is and will be', which can lift the veils of Isis. And it is the 'I' that does this by transforming intelligence. Our ordinary intelligence comprehends only the finished work of the gods, the earthly world that lies all around us. When it is transformed into Imagination we perceive the effects of divine forces; at the next stage, Inspiration, we receive the revelation of the gods; finally, in Intuition, we are reunited with divine being, with the powers that were and are and will be. The upward path of the human individuality and of intelligence coincide.

There exists a poem written by a Gnostic Christian around the second century called the 'Hymn of the Pearl'.[1] It describes the process outlined above in the form of a story about a young prince who grows up in a marvellous palace under the care of his devoted royal parents. When he reaches adulthood the prince is sent away on a mission that he must accomplish alone. In a far-off land called Egypt a pearl lies hidden in the depths of a lake guarded by a serpent. His task is to return with this pearl. The young man makes the long journey. He finds the lake and succeeds in obtaining the pearl, but as he sets out on his return journey he encounters a group of young Egyptians. He is drawn to them and accepts their customs; he even starts

6. THE ACTIVITY OF MICHAEL

dressing like them. Soon the young prince has forgotten who he is and why he came to Egypt in the first place. He has fallen into bad company, and in time he becomes destitute and filled with despair. His parents have not forgotten him, however, and they send him an eagle with a letter that reads: 'Remember that you are the son of a king and your parents anxiously await for your return.' The young prince awakens as though from an evil dream and returns home to his parents, bringing with him the precious pearl.

In the story, the land of Egypt is the symbol for earthly existence, the pearl represents freedom, and the letter reminding the young man of his true nature is thinking, intelligence. The young man is every one of us. The poem, although written in the epoch of the intellectual soul, is a prophetic vision of humanity's situation in the age of the consciousness soul.

The pearl of freedom, hidden in the dark depth of our will forces, where also the serpent of passions and desires live, cannot be brought back without 'reading the letter', in other words without the means of thinking and intelligence. A letter is an apt symbol for our thoughts. The gods do not speak directly to us any longer; instead they have to communicate through letters, dead signs on dead paper. But just as in real life a letter from a friend, even though it consists only of signs on paper, can bring them near to us, so too our clear concepts can and should make us realise that we are spirits, thereby setting us on the road to our divine origin. The letter is brought by an eagle, which is another symbol for the power of thinking. The Gnostic poem presents in the form of images what the Michael Letter expresses in concepts suitable for the age of the consciousness soul: that thinking is the means, the only means, that can lead us, in freedom, back to the gods from whom we came.

Michael is the cosmic steward of thinking, and it was cosmic thought, or as we can call it, Cosmic Intelligence, that created the order of our planetary system out of chaos. What we observe as rhythms in the movement of the sun, moon and planets is the result of this Cosmic Intelligence. But the gods whose thoughts designed this planetary system are no longer present in it, nor are the stars in their courses any longer a manifestation or revelation of the gods. Just as humanity on earth is removed three stages from the world of being and lives in the world of finished work, so the cosmic order is removed two stages and is a world of the effects of the gods.

Michael regards it as his task to connect humanity with the order of the cosmos in a particular way. When human souls enter earthly existence they do so in harmony with the course of the sun, moon and planets: this is the secret of true astrology and of the individual horoscope. It is Michael's deed that we are born at a time when the position of the planets is in harmony with the karmic disposition of our souls.

Why does Michael concern himself with the task of bringing about this harmony? When people in our time are interested in astrology they generally consider the matter only from a narrow, selfish point of view. No one would be inclined to ask: what does it mean for the cosmos, for the sun, moon and planets that we are connected with them when we enter earthly existence? But it does mean something, because in each one of us there is something which is of a divine nature, a spiritual being just as the gods, our 'Fathers in Heaven', are spiritual beings. It is this spiritual being in us that continuously renews and gives life to the planetary spheres which, by themselves, are already two stages removed from the world of being, the world of the gods. This is the reason why Michael, who once established the cosmic order, derives such deep satisfaction from the connection he has made between humanity and the cosmos. In the words of the sixth Letter, 'this deed gives him such deep satisfaction that in it he finds a portion of his very life, a portion of his sunlike, living energy'.

One is used to finding in Rudolf Steiner's work ideas that must strike the reader as bewildering. But few of these are so contrary to our thought habits as the concept presented in this Michael Letter: that human beings confer a boon upon

The Old Man with the Lamp

Goethe's Fairy Tale

An Angel Being

Slumbering Figure

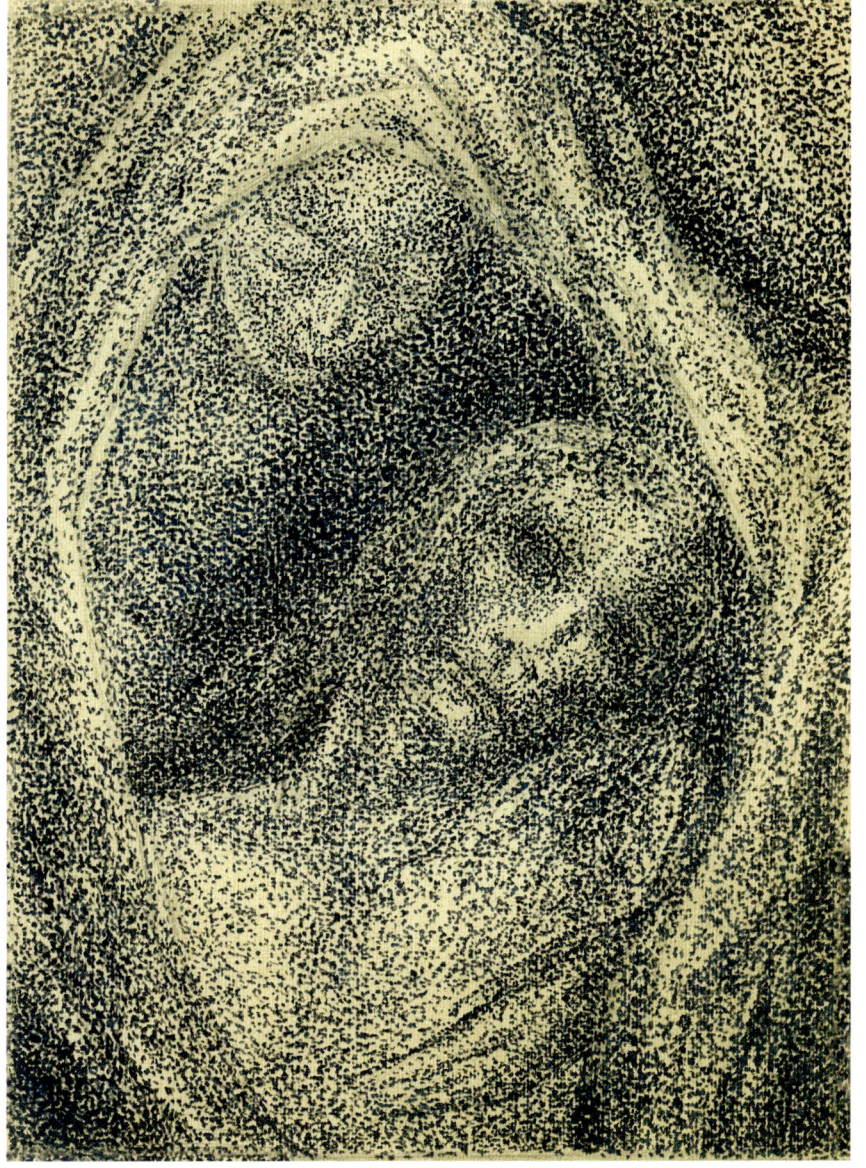

Pietà

Pietà

Gethsemane

'May this cup be taken from me'

The Dance of the Elves

The Goddess Natura

St Christopher

The Angel of Death

Michael

Michael

The Baptism in the Jordan

Christ Jesus

6. THE ACTIVITY OF MICHAEL

the cosmos by linking their descent into earthly incarnation to the patterns formed by the movements of the planets. Yet this picture of the human being's relation to the cosmos is not so difficult to accept if we recall the Gnostic poem and the message its hero received: 'Remember that you are the son of a king'. We are of divine nature, and while this godlike element in us has, of necessity, only a limited scope on Earth, it can and, through Michael, does work in the cosmic realms through which we pass on our descent to earth.

The cosmos we see above us in all its majesty is growing old. Not only earthly organisms are subject to the ageing process: the universe as a whole is wearing out just as our physical body does as we get old. But just as the ageing body contains the forces to build a new body in the next life, so the ageing cosmos contains the forces to build the world of the future. They exist already in humanity. And they exist there because Christ has united himself with humanity. In as far as we carry the Christ impulse with us into the life between death and a new birth, we bestow on the cosmic spheres this spiritual life which otherwise has already withdrawn from them.

This thought leads us to another aspect of humanity's relationship to the cosmos. In his book *The Spiritual Guidance of the Individual and Humanity*, Rudolf Steiner says that when a child is born their etheric brain receives an impression of the sky above as it is at the moment of birth, rather like a photograph of the starry heavens.[2] This is, as Rudolf Steiner points out, the reality on which true astrology is based. As we learn from this sixth Michael Letter, it is a reality that is due to Michael. Rudolf Steiner then goes on to speak about the baptism in the Jordan. From this baptism, and throughout the three years of the life of the Christ Jesus, there was in him at every moment such a 'photograph' of the stars. What happens to us only once, at the moment of birth, happened continually while Christ Jesus was on Earth. What is the meaning of such a revelation? It means that whatever Christ did or said in any moment of his earthly life was in harmony with the cosmos.

Or, to put it another way, we can say that whatever Christ said or did was said or done 'at the right time'.

Time is not merely an abstract flow of seconds, minutes and hours; it is a music that flows on without a break. Every moment in this unending symphony is a specific accord, and none of these accords or harmonies will ever be repeated again. The birth of a baby takes place (assuming there is no human interference) when it is the right time for that particular soul. In the case of the Christ Jesus, every word and every deed was such a 'birth' at the right time: all was in harmony with the great symphony of the heavens.

Beside our moment of birth, in which we have little say in any case as far as our earthly consciousness is concerned, are we ordinary mortals ever in a position to act in harmony with the cosmic symphony? According to Rudolf Steiner, the answer is yes, whenever we act out of moral intuition. This is a term he used in *The Philosophy of Freedom* and refers to acts carried out in complete freedom. When we can free ourselves from all conventions, from all urges arising from our lower nature, from the compulsions of custom and habit and act out of our innermost self, then we act in complete harmony with the stars above us as they are in this moment. This is why, as Steiner stated in *The Philosophy of Freedom*, there can be no universal moral code for human beings who act out of true freedom. As the patterns formed by the stars change, so morality changes and what is considered 'good' today can be 'evil' tomorrow.

Christ Jesus was 'good' all the time because he acted at every moment in harmony with the changing patterns of the stars – his every step was formed out of a moral intuition. And this is what is given by Christ to all human beings on earth: if we act out of our innermost self, we act in harmony with the cosmic order as it is at that precise moment. We act out of moral intuition.

But intuition is not possible without thinking. It is only in pure thought, a thought free from instincts and unconscious urges, from conventions and traditions, that one can receive

6. THE ACTIVITY OF MICHAEL

moral intuitions. And it is here that we once more encounter Michael, the cosmic steward of thinking. It is Michael who connects us with the stars when we descend into earthly life, and he also connects us with the stars in moral intuitions. When this happens, impulses are born on Earth in which the cosmos and human beings are one, as they were in the beginning and as they are at the birth of a child.

7

The Michael-Christ Experience of Humanity

November 9, 1924

The seventh Michael Letter aims to make clear the meaning of living in a world that is the finished work of the gods, but in which they are no longer present. It is a situation that has two consequences. First of all, any knowledge of the world of Nature can only make us aware of the *past* creative deeds of the gods. The reality of the divine world is no more in surrounding Nature than Raphael is personally present when you look at one of his paintings. The picture will tell you something of the genius who created it, but the genius himself has departed. Of course there are elemental beings active in Nature, there are etheric and astral forces, but they are not creators, they merely repeat designs created by divine intelligences in past stages of world evolution. Secondly, because there is no divine reality present in the world around us, we cannot learn from Nature anything about our own true human nature. More importantly we cannot learn from Nature how to act in a truly human fashion – Nature is not moral.

This division is reflected in philosophy, which recognises two kinds of concepts: cognitive and moral. Cognitive concepts help us understand the world around us, such as the concepts found in physics, chemistry or biology, whereas moral concepts apply only to human behaviour in such things as truthfulness and compassion. What appears in philosophy in a more abstract fashion shows itself in a more tangible form in the split between science and religion. Science seeks a knowledge of the world of Nature that excludes any moral judgments; religion is concerned with moral values that have significance only for humans, not for anything in Nature. The inevitable consequence of this division was that the Church declared that the spiritual revelations contained in the Bible were far above the thinking and reasoning we employ to comprehend earthly matters. This spiritual revelation had to be accepted by faith. On the other hand, scientists came more and more to the conclusion that the Old Testament and the New Testament were the products of a pre-scientific, superstitious age and that those ancient legends contained nothing compatible with scientific knowledge.

This polarisation, which is now a fact of contemporary life, developed only gradually. In the sixteenth and early seventeenth centuries, when this process was still in its beginning, there were people who foresaw that the coming division would have far-reaching consequences, depending on which side would gain the upper hand. The winning side would determine the social order of the future. The people who took this long view and planned accordingly were the Jesuits and the Freemasons. The Jesuits aimed for a social order in which the Church of Rome would become the worldwide authority on all things spiritual, thereby controlling people's conscience and their actions. The Freemasons pursued a seemingly more democratic social order in which people would act in accordance with the rational thinking fostered by science. Meanwhile, spiritual knowledge would become the preserve of a small group who would be in a position to manipulate others from behind the scenes. It may seem paradoxical, but it is really so that one could say the Jesuits invented socialism and the Freemasons modern capitalism.

7. THE MICHAEL-CHRIST EXPERIENCE

As absurd and fantastic as it sounds, the materialistic, atheistic socialism of Soviet Russia was not at all contrary to the intentions of the Jesuits. The Communists after all suppressed Rome's competitor, the Russian Orthodox Church. But in the long run, the soulless ideology of Marxism could not satisfy the souls of such intensively religious people as the Russians. America is already the citadel of capitalism. It is also the country in which technology, the practical fruit of scientific thinking, has progressed faster and further than anywhere else. Masonic Lodges are all-pervading, and hidden manipulators work through them. Such superpowers seek world domination and what results can only be an uneasy, perilous balance of terror.

This division, which we know as an all too tangible physical reality, was only the outcome of the spiritual situation outlined at the beginning: human beings, who are spiritual beings, finds themselves in a world in which there is no living spirit present. The East–West confrontation that once dominated the global stage showed the Ahrimanic and Luciferic aberrations to which Rudolf Steiner refers in this Michael Letter. The socialism of the East was an Ahrimanic distortion of a social form that belongs to the future, whereas the capitalism of the West preserves a Luciferic selfishness that was a necessary stage of human evolution in the past but can, in the present age, bring only chaos and disaster. We must not forget, however, that there is in every one of us a capitalist whose actions are determined by self-interest, and a socialist who desires the help and support of a community. The world at large presents only an image of the division within each soul.

This Michael Letter serves as a signpost indicating the direction in which we must travel in order to heal this rift, first of all within ourselves, but also in world affairs. As stated before, the natural world around us contains no spiritual presence, but it speaks everywhere of the divine spiritual powers who, in past stages of evolution, created it. It is one of Michael's concerns that we learn to understand the language in which the world speaks to us. Michael wants human souls to read in the Book of Nature as it is described in the Leading Thoughts.

Goethe's Theory of Colour can serve as an indication for such a 'reading in the Book of Nature'. Goethe regarded the colours of the spectrum – as we see them in a rainbow, but also if light passes through a glass prism – as the result of a struggle between light and darkness. In yellow the light is stronger; in blue it is the darkness. In red both forces exert their maximum strength but hold each other in balance; in green there is also a balance but with both forces at rest. It is not surprising that established science has, to this day, simply disregarded this interpretation of colour, as there is no observable 'struggle' or 'fight' in the colour phenomena of the spectrum. Yet Goethe was right: the colours are the result of a battle between light and darkness, but a battle that took place during the ancient Moon evolution. In the first stages of that evolution there was only one planetary body. Then the Sun, and its host of higher spiritual beings, departed and became a separate shining body, leaving the Moon without any light of its own.

This was the first moment in evolution when light and darkness confronted each other and when, through this confrontation, colours could arise. But the separation of the Sun was the result of the War in Heaven, a battle between the Spirits of Movement who had evolved at the right pace and those who had fallen behind. This War in Heaven is the spiritual origin of colour, but it is a war that was fought in a distant past. And this ancient war between spiritual beings had a moral quality too in the sense that will forces clashed with one another.

Goethe did not see in colours the bloodless vibrations at different wavelengths described by modern science. Instead, he experienced in the sense impressions the sensual and moral effects of colours (*sinnlich-sittliche Wirkung der Farbe*), the moral quality of the past. There is something else that follows from such a way of looking at the phenomena of colour. As a result

7. THE MICHAEL-CHRIST EXPERIENCE

of the battle on ancient Moon between the spirits of light and the spirits of darkness, we now perceive colours in nature: the rainbow, sunset and sunrise, the colours of the plants and of precious stones. They all are here because there was once a purely spiritual battle, a battle which no physical eye could have seen. And there is again another battle between light and darkness in every human soul. It is not a battle that physical eyes can see, but the results of this invisible battle will become part of our natural environment in future stages of world evolution, not as colours this time but as pleasant or unpleasant smells.[1]

Our moral life will become outer Nature in worlds of the future, just as the present Nature around us is the result of the moral life of other, higher beings in the past. But the ultimate significance of reading in the Book of Nature, in the Michaelic sense, can be understood if we consider the following facts of human history. In ancient times when humanity still lived in tribal societies, young people listened to songs and epic poems telling them of the great deeds of some ancestor-hero. It was by hearing of their ancestors that young people felt inspired to become worthy of them. The reason these sagas survived for centuries and were passed on from generation to generation was precisely because they were a source of such inspiration. In our time the blood ties of tribal life have lost their strength, and nothing could be worse for us now than emulating our physical ancestors. We have become individuals, and what we need is a knowledge that connects us with our spiritual ancestors – it is their deeds that can inspire us. And their deeds are spread out all around us as the world of Nature. Looking out at Nature as Goethe did, and learning through anthroposophy of the deeds of the hierarchies on ancient Saturn, Sun, Moon and the beginning of Earth evolution, these can become the sources of inspiration for our time. This is the direction in which Michael wants to guide us.

In ancient tribal society the wish to be worthy of the ancestors was fostered by sagas, but the strength to translate mere wishes into deeds, into one's personal conduct, came through inherited instincts in the blood. In our time this strength cannot be found in any genetic inheritance. We must seek the Christ in order to find in him, as free individuals, the power to transform ideals into deeds, wishes into actions, and intentions into facts. The strength of soul thus gained in striving toward the Christ protects us against the temptation to become part of the herd or the mob, to surrender to the socialist in us. And the understanding of the world gained on the path of knowledge to which we are directed by Michael extinguishes the illusion that we can achieve anything by and for ourselves alone. What we do only has value in as far as it contributes to the evolution of humanity. This disposes of the capitalist in us.

Rudolf Steiner speaks at the end of this Letter of the Michael-Christ path on which we are meant to travel. It is the road already shown in *The Philosophy of Freedom*. The first half of the book deals with thinking as a means of understanding the world. This is the part inspired by Michael. In the second half, thinking is shown as the means by which we receive moral intuitions, and love as the power that enables us to carry these intuitions into our will. In this part of the book there speaks the Christ impulse.

To the ordinary reader this book may seem to be no more than one philosophic thesis amongst many others. Anthroposophists, however, should recognise it as the beginning of the Michael-Christ path.

8

Michael's Mission in the Cosmic Age of Human Freedom

November 16, 1924

The eighth Michael Letter contains a passage that is especially difficult to understand and must be studied closely. It is the passage that describes the particular relationship that must exist between the physical body, the etheric body, the astral body and the 'I' in order for human freedom to be possible.

Unless we are fully conscious we cannot act out of freedom, and we are not fully conscious unless the 'I' and the astral body are united with the etheric and physical bodies. When this is not the case, when the 'I' and astral body are separated from the etheric and physical bodies, then we are unconscious, we are asleep. However, according to Rudolf Steiner in this letter, freedom is only possible if on the one hand the lower, unconscious part of ourselves (the etheric and physical bodies) do not affect the higher, conscious parts (the 'I' and astral body), and on the other if the higher parts do not interfere with the lower.

The etheric and physical bodies are the bearers of instinctive forces such as growth, digestion and reproduction, and these must not exert an influence on our waking consciousness or else we are not free. Likewise, the 'I' and the astral body, which are created to be free, must not carry the arbitrary nature of our conscious life into the harmonious working of the instinctive forces. If they did, it would be harmful to our health.

The conditions necessary for freedom are therefore somewhat contradictory: the two aspects of the human totality must be together yet must not affect each other. It is something that cannot and does not happen naturally. When it does happen it is a miracle in the most literal sense of the word. Rudolf Steiner hinted at this mystery when he once said that any truly moral deed, by which he meant a free deed, is a miracle.[1] The being that makes this miracle possible is Christ, working through his servant Michael.

The process as described in this letter is the following: when we act in freedom, we unconsciously repel certain instinctive forces in the etheric and physical bodies. These forces are of a cosmic nature and would make us act in accordance with the cosmos, but in doing so they would make us unfree. At the same time Michael replaces these suppressed forces with the forces he has through his connection with the Christ being. This is the nature of the miracle of our freedom: the natural, instinctive forces are suppressed and are replaced instead from a higher, purely spiritual source.

To understand what is implied by this complicated procedure we should ask ourselves what kind of instinctive forces are suppressed or repelled during the first step of this process. They are the forces of reproduction, the instinctive love-forces in human beings, and they are replaced by love for an ideal, by a purely spiritual love. Through the forces of physical love children are conceived; through the forces of spiritual love the human being conceives ideas for moral impulses and moral deeds. Both conceptions are manifestations of love. But whereas in physical conception love is the instrument of the Moon powers, in spiritual conception love is a gift of the Sun powers: Michael-Christ.

There was a time when, in preparation for the Mystery of Golgotha, the Moon-god Yahweh was both the ruler of the forces of reproduction and the moral law-giver of the people

8. MICHAEL'S MISSION IN THE AGE OF FREEDOM

chosen for this purpose – the Jews. At that time the divine beings had not yet withdrawn from the world of Nature, and so in the Old Testament Yahweh reveals himself through his power over natural events. It is Yahweh who brings about the Great Flood that destroys Atlantis. It is he who sends the ten plagues over Egypt and who parts the Red Sea for the Israelites to pass. These and many other instances show Yahweh as a god who commands the forces of Nature. But it is also Yahweh who gives Moses the Ten Commandments and, with them, the laws of human morality as they were to be at that time.

Yahweh worked in and through the instincts of the people. Through him human beings had an instinctive feeling for whether an action was right or wrong. Of course, it was a tribal, or racial, morality that he inspired, an ethos as harsh and as unforgiving as the laws of Nature themselves. But the Ten Commandments pronounced on Mount Sinai (speaking to the consciousness of human beings) and the powerful instincts for what was right or wrong (working from the unconscious of human beings) gave people direction in life, strength in adversity, and a faith in a divine world order that modern humanity has lost forever.

Yahweh, the Moon-god, who spoke on Mount Sinai in thunder and lightning, who directed and guided the tribal instincts and who directs the forces of reproduction, is also the god whom Michael served before the Mystery of Golgotha. Since then he has become a servant of the Sun Spirit, who united himself with the Earth. Now the instinctive forces must be overcome, must give way to the forces of spiritual love.

A special instance – and one singled out by Rudolf Steiner – is the sense of duty. Most of us would still regard a sense of duty as a positive trait, but in a lecture given on November 22, 1914, Rudolf Steiner spoke about a negative aspect of duty.[2] In this instance Ahriman holds sway and, under his influence, people become slaves to duty, following in a cold and rigid way rules that have been set by some authority. Steiner had already attacked the validity of duty as a moral principle in

The Philosophy of Freedom. Nothing demonstrates more clearly how right and far-seeing he was when, in the aftermath of the Second World War, members of the SS accused of atrocities in concentration camps defended themselves by saying they were only following orders, they were only doing their duty.

The sense of duty that most people would regard as a virtue is really an instinct, one that was necessary at a time when individuals felt themselves to be more a part of a group. Then, loyalty to the group and the faithful observance of the rules that governed the life of that group, were essential for human existence. The duty-instinct is a remnant of this time. It is one of the instincts governed by Yahweh, the Moon-god, and the Jews of ancient times regarded a person as virtuous, or righteous, if they dutifully observed the rules laid down by Yahweh through his servant, Moses. At the time of Jesus, the Pharisees were representative of this obedient attitude to God. But it was the Pharisee Saul who, as Paul, renounced the concept of duty towards divine law and proclaimed a new principle: love. This is also what Rudolf Steiner emphasises in the lecture mentioned above when he speaks about the effects of the coming of the etheric Christ. In place of duty Christ will bring a love for one's task, for when the motive is love there is no compulsion and no duty. This theme is also central to the second part of *The Philosophy of Freedom*.

We live at a time when the duty-instinct, like much else that belonged to the condition of the group soul, is fading away, while the new love impulse is still very weak. Many of the social problems of the present have their roots in the fact that we live in an in-between time, but we should be aware that it is part of Michael's task to prevent the old instincts from continuing as they did in the past. They could make people virtuous or righteous in the sense in which the Pharisees were virtuous. Yet they were the people whom Christ denounced again and again. Michael is suppressing Saul, the Pharisee in us, so that there is room for Paul, the Christian.

In ancient times, when Yahweh was the power that gave

8. MICHAEL'S MISSION IN THE AGE OF FREEDOM

people moral directions, it was Lucifer who tempted human souls to transgress those rules. The Old Testament tells the story of the manifold transgressions of the Jewish people and their leaders, and of the grim warnings of the prophets. Lucifer was then the spirit who wanted to free human souls from bondage to the Law of Yahweh. The same battle is at the core of some of the great works of literature. Consider the stories of Romeo and Juliet, Tristan and Isolde, Paris and Helen: these tales are all of unlawful love, love that breaks the rules of the society in which the lovers live – the rules of the Moon-god.

Today these rules are either openly disregarded or observed only as formalities. The divine forces which once lived in these rules have withdrawn from them as they have withdrawn from Nature around us. In the ancient past, reproduction was the sacred preserve of Yahweh. Today sex is a flourishing industry and pornography is a form of business earning millions. This time it is Ahriman who has taken over and who wants to keep people in bondage by means of the depraved sex forces.

The only power that can heal this sickness is the true, unconditional, spiritual love that Paul called *agapē*,[3] the love whose source is the Sun Spirit.

9

World-thoughts in the Working of Michael and in the Working of Ahriman

November 23, 1924

In the ninth Michael Letter we are presented with imaginations that are meant to lead us to an understanding of the nature of Michael compared with the nature of Ahriman. One might think that anthroposophists who have studied Rudolf Steiner's work for many years could make this distinction with ease, but this is not necessarily the case; we are all prone to let Ahriman think in us and for us without even noticing it. Here Rudolf Steiner's warning should be heeded that it is quite possible for two spiritual beings to say the same thing, but one is a good being and the other evil. In the case of Michael and Ahriman the distinction is made all the more difficult as they have one thing in common: a connection to cosmic thoughts or, as it is also called, Cosmic Intelligence. That is why we are well advised to let our minds dwell on the contents and imaginations of this Michael Letter. They can make us more perceptive for the differences between the two antagonists and more on guard against the persuasive power of Ahriman's thoughts.

Both Michael and Ahriman have 'cosmic intelligence'. What does this mean? The following comparison can help us to come to an understanding. Imagine first of all a performance by a group of eurythmists. Every one of the performers on the stage moves about in a particular way, but all the different movements are in harmony with one another. The eurythmists do not collide, although there is no one individual who directs their movements. Now compare this with the flow of traffic in a busy road. It has to be regulated by traffic lights if serious accidents are to be avoided. Here too the movements are directed, but by an outside mechanical system. In both cases intelligence was used to create order out of chaos.

In the living order of a eurythmy performance there is something akin to the Michael intelligence; in the mechanical regulation of the traffic we can recognise a similarity to Ahriman's intelligence. We can also realise that there is a necessity for this Ahrimanic order in the conditions of the present age: when the horse was still the only means of locomotion there was no need for traffic signals. Having understood the difference between the two kinds of order we can now take the next step and consider a particular kind of order in which both kinds of intelligence coincide. It is the order of the movements of sun, moon and planets in the cosmos.

On the one hand it is so mechanical that astronomers can calculate the position of any cosmic body, where it was a hundred years ago, where it will be a hundred years from now. The planets move with clockwork precision, and because they do, astronomers assume that these calculable movements are all there is to the planets. But there is more to it, and this 'more' reveals itself in the rhythms of Nature around us, in the working of our organs in the body and in each human destiny on Earth. This inner cosmic life, hidden behind the calculable order, is the realm of Michael's intelligence.

Few things illustrate the two intelligences better than the two ways in which we can look upon the cosmic rhythm of the year. We can either take account of the simple fact that certain holidays fall upon certain dates and plan our work and leisure time accordingly, or we can try to live with the spiritual realities

9. WORLD-THOUGHTS IN THE WORKING OF MICHAEL

of the seasons by following the verses of the *Calendar of the Soul* by Rudolf Steiner, or at least approach the yearly festivals with the right inner mood. The first attitude is forced upon us. We have no choice but to accept that on certain days shops will be closed and fewer buses will run. In this we can recognise the hand of Ahriman. It lies in our freedom, however, to choose to adopt the other attitude and to inwardly cultivate it. One can recognise from this simple illustration that Ahriman is the arch-philistine in us, who looks upon all things with an eye only for their utility, whereas the Michaelic attitude nurtures an interest in all things for their own sake, regardless of how useful they are.

And this is just what Rudolf Steiner describes in this letter as the difference between Michael's and Ahriman's relationship to the Cosmic Intelligence. Ahriman wants to use it for himself to expand his own power, whereas Michael selflessly reflects the pure wisdom of the divine powers who gave existence to the world, humanity and to Michael himself. Michael looks upon this wisdom with reverence; Ahriman calculates its usefulness. If one contemplates Michael's attitude to the Cosmic Intelligence there arises, almost by itself, an understanding of what Rudolf Steiner means when he describes Michael's earnest countenance, the earnest look in his eyes.

A person who enters a building which they regard as holy, a church or a temple, will not offend the dignity of this sacred place by laughing or chattering; they will conduct themselves with the seriousness which their religious conviction calls for. Michael is forever in the presence of the divine wisdom, a wisdom that is not an abstract thought structure but a living reality. How could his attitude be anything other than deeply serious, deeply earnest? We human beings are not used to treating the thoughts which come into our minds with great respect, and that is quite right. They are, for the most part, not of a kind to be taken very seriously at all. It is different, however, for a spiritual being of the rank of Michael. He sees his thoughts as World-thoughts, as the Cosmic Intelligence of gods who are as far above him as he is above us. Before such thoughts he stands in awe, in reverence, and beholds them in deep earnestness.

There was at least one human being to whom it was given through Michael to see what Michael sees, to behold the glory of the divine wisdom. This was Rudolf Steiner, and in his face, in his eyes, we can see that same deep earnestness. To be sure, he would laugh and joke with friends and especially with children; he could be joyful and was, by nature, an optimist. But one only has to look at his eyes in all the photographs that exist of him to realise the profound seriousness which never left him even in moments of happiness. It is the earnestness of those (whether they are human or angelic beings) who live in the presence of the divine wisdom. The earnestness in the eyes of Rudolf Steiner is the earthly reflection of the earnestness of Michael in the spiritual world.

This earnest expression in the eyes of Rudolf Steiner has also great significance for the future. In the lectures about the karma of the anthroposophical movement we are told that true anthroposophists will in their next incarnation have certain features in common: there will be a certain resemblance in their faces, independent of any national or racial characteristics. What could this resemblance be? Surely nothing else than a resemblance to what we can already see in the eyes, in the face, of Rudolf Steiner. This is only natural because, for true anthroposophists, Michael will take over the position of our national folk-soul who at present moulds the basic elements of our features. Michael will be the folk-soul of the anthroposophists of the future and they will then, here on Earth, resemble him as Rudolf Steiner did in his earthly life. But this can only happen insofar as we have begun, in the present earthly life, to develop that attitude to the World-thoughts that Michael has. These World-thoughts are given to us in the form of anthroposophy. They are, to begin with, no more than printed words in books. But if we try to penetrate more deeply into them, these thoughts come alive in us and then we have to

9. WORLD-THOUGHTS IN THE WORKING OF MICHAEL

learn to stand before them in reverence – to treat our thinking about anthroposophical concepts with the same earnestness as a religious person feels when saying a heartfelt prayer. It is not the quantity of our knowledge but the seriousness with which we treat the little we do know that brings us nearer to Michael, the future archangelic folk-soul. It is this serious attitude which will in the next incarnation mould the faces of those who are connected with him.[1]

What Michael beholds and what gives his countenance the grave expression, so we are told in this letter, are the World-thoughts of the Cosmic Intelligence. We have already been made aware that the movements of the sun, moon and planets are an expression of this intelligence, but these movements, which we observe from Earth, are only the 'outer' aspects of these heavenly bodies. They are no more than signs, but we must ask ourselves what these signs mean.

In the lectures he gave on the karma of the anthroposophical movement, Rudolf Steiner made a statement that answers this question, perhaps one of the briefest formulations in his whole work. He said that the Cosmic Intelligence is nothing less than the interrelationship of the higher hierarchies, the continually changing relationships that exist between the beings of different ranks, between the Angels and the Spirits of Movement, or between the Archangels and the Spirits of Form and the Spirits of Wisdom: all the manifold variations in which the nine hierarchies work together.[2] These deeds are woven together in a great symphony, what Pythagoras called the Music of the Spheres, and this is what is meant by the Cosmic Intelligence. Of this majestic music, we see no more than the slow movements of the planets in their orbits. It is only after death that we experience the reality behind these celestial phenomena, of which most people take hardly any notice.

Michael is part of this symphony or intelligence, but he is also the being who is privileged to behold at the same time the glory and power of it all. We human souls, too, are part of it in life after death. But during life on earth we are meant to learn to understand this divine intelligence, which means to behold it in our thinking. This is the task of anthroposophy. Without anthroposophy, human intelligence will be completely cut off from its cosmic origin and will be absorbed by Ahriman. For the future of humanity's evolution the philistine thinking emanating from Ahriman is a far greater threat than the many things which fill people with anxiety in our time. The imaginations of this Michael Letter can awaken us to this threat.

10

At the Gates of the Consciousness Soul

November 30, 1924

The previous Michael Letters were concerned with portraying Michael as a cosmic being: they show him as the steward of the Cosmic Intelligence. When this intelligence has descended into the physical realm, where human beings can use or misuse it, Michael sees it as his task to keep human beings connected through this intelligence to the gods of their origin. Not feelings, not belief, but the understanding that can only be gained by using the intelligence given to us in the age of the consciousness soul: this is what Michael expects from us.

However, the tenth letter turns to quite another aspect of Michael. It describes his working in human history over the last 800 years. We know that it was only towards the end of the nineteenth century that Michael became the ruling Time Spirit for a period of about 300 years. But Michael had been preparing for his present rulership for many centuries before the time came for him to guide human destiny once more. This preparation can be traced by considering certain phenomena that are characteristic of the twelfth, thirteenth and fourteenth centuries, the period before the age of the consciousness soul began.

This was when the ancient instinctive faculty of imagination was on the wane and the new intellectual faculty of sharply defined concepts was still in its infancy. It was this twilight in human consciousness that produced the sagas, legends and fairy tales that have come down to us from the Middle Ages. They are not mythology and not history; they are not imaginary nor are they fact. They are not true in the sense that we might expect an eyewitness account of some event to be true, but they are true if we understand that they refer to a spiritual reality.

Rudolf Steiner retells one of these sagas at great length in this Michael Letter. Considering that he was at that time already very ill and that he kept his communications in the Michael Letters as brief as possible, it should come as a surprise that in this letter he fills several pages with the story of Gerhard the Good. Unless this story of a good person contained some profound truth, the time he gave to writing out this old fable would have been wasted, which was not Rudolf Steiner's way, least of all in the last months of his life. We have, therefore, to regard the saga of Gerhard the Good as much more than an edifying tale for children.

Gerhard is a trader, a businessman who travels far and wide to obtain his merchandise. He sails to the far north to buy furs and to the far south to get silks and velvet. Having acquired goods that can be sold very profitably in his hometown of Cologne, he gives all his wares away as a ransom to buy the freedom of some Christian knights held prisoner by a heathen king.

Among the prisoners freed by Gerhard there is also a princess, the bride of King William of England. No one knows what happened to the king and it is assumed that he died on a pilgrimage. Gerhard takes the princess to his home in Cologne, where she is treated as if she were his own daughter. Gerhard has a son who would like to marry the beautiful visitor, but the father insists that he waits a full year in case the English king turns up. The year is past and the wedding is about to be held

10. AT THE GATES OF THE CONSCIOUSNESS SOUL

when a poor pilgrim arrives. He is King William. Gerhard is not only happy to see the king reunited with his bride but helps King William regain his kingdom; he subsequently refuses any reward or compensation.

The story contains already in its beginning the key to its understanding. Who or what is it that travels far north and far south? It is the sun in the course of the year. It moves northward from Christmas to Midsummer and then moves south in the other six months. Gerhard represents a Sun-being, the Sun-archangel Michael. He gives all he has to free the Christian knights. This is the image for Michael's concern with human freedom. The heathen king who had captured the knights is Ahriman. Only Michael, giving what he has, the Cosmic Intelligence, can set them free. We have already seen from the previous letter that Michael is utterly selfless in his stewardship of the Cosmic Intelligence.

The princess is the consciousness soul. The European country that was destined to develop these particular soul forces was (and still is) Britain, which has always been called England on the continent. At the time when the story of Gerhard the Good was written, the age of the consciousness soul had not yet begun. The bride had to wait until the folk-soul of the British Isles could be united with her.

The age of the consciousness soul began in the fifteenth century when the spring equinox entered the constellation of Pisces, a water sign. It was in the fifteenth century that the great voyages of discovery began and, for the first time, ships sailed around the globe. This was also the beginning of world trade, and while we may take a somewhat negative view of business and business practices, there is another aspect to global trade. Through their travels, merchants connected far-flung regions and people, and through their buying and selling they brought about a world that is, economically, a oneness, a unit. Business is, by its very nature, international and cosmopolitan, and thus works in the direction of the Michael impulse. At present the selfishness of individuals and nations hides the true mission of trade, which is to recognise that all human beings depend on each other. But the time will come when selfishness in economic life will be seen for what it really is: a fatal illness. Gerhard the Good represents the trader of the future, the bearer of the cosmopolitan Michael impulse. The tale of the selfless trader was written at a time when feuding warlords were still making history, but what announced itself in that saga was a vision of the future as Michael sees it. This is the reason why Rudolf Steiner found the story important enough to include in this letter.

The dreamlike imagination which produced the Gerhard fable also created the other saga mentioned in this letter: the adventures of the Duke Ernst. Here the deeper meaning of the tale is already indicated by the name of the hero. In the previous letter we have read of the earnest gaze of Michael. It is therefore no accident that in the next letter we meet a knight whose name implies a connection with this spiritual being. The Duke represents another aspect of Michael.

Duke Ernst and his companions are shipwrecked on the Magnet Mountain, a mountain that attracts ships with a magnetic force. When the ships strike the rocks they are shattered. The Duke and his men find the shore littered with the bodies of men and animals that have perished from hunger and thirst after escaping death by drowning. But the knights also observe enormous birds, called gryphons, which pick up corpses and fly them to their nests to eat. The Duke decides to make use of these monstrous birds. He and his friends skin some of the dead animals and wrap the skins around themselves. The gryphons come, take them to be the usual carrion and carry them to their nests far inland. When the birds fly away again to gather more food, the knights throw off the hides and proceed on their journey.

One could hardly find a better image for the way in which Ahriman works than the Magnet Mountain with its deadly power of attraction. The Gryphon, on the other hand, represents the Luciferic forces. What Duke Ernst does is

10. AT THE GATES OF THE CONSCIOUSNESS SOUL

use Lucifer against Ahriman in order to save his men from destruction by either force. This is the way that the Michael-Christ impulse works: by keeping a balance between Ahriman and Lucifer.

The same theme is expressed in other episodes of the saga. The travellers come to a country where there are people with ears so big that they can wrap them around their bodies like cloaks. We can actually see such a figure in the form of Lucifer on the right-hand side of Christ in the wooden sculpture at the Goetheanum. There Lucifer's ears are so big that they have become wing-like organs which surround the body like a billowing cloak. The land of the people with large ears is the realm of Lucifer.

In another country visited by the Duke and his knights, the feet of the inhabitants are so large that when it rains they stand on their heads and use their feet as umbrellas. The human foot is the part of the body that is in closest contact with the earth; its form is specially adapted to the earth-forces. Beings who use what is of an earthly nature to shield themselves against the cosmos, to cut themselves off from the cosmos, belong to the realm of Ahriman. By visiting these two kinds of beings, one of which has part of the head over-developed, the other, part of the limbs, Duke Ernst again balances the two forces against each other and so shows himself as representing the Michael impulse.

Both tales, Gerhard the Good and Duke Ernst, are imaginative descriptions of the way the Michael powers operate. They are told as if they were describing physical events, thus demonstrating the twilight consciousness that prevailed in the centuries preceding the age of the consciousness soul. Michael, the spirit of clarity, had to disperse this spiritual fog by turning the human being's attention to the sense world with its clear outlines and sharp details – he used Ahriman to defy Lucifer. This is the deeper reason why modern science had to come: to give human beings the opportunity to develop clear thinking. Once this has been gained it can be raised to the level of understanding spiritual truth (as well as obscure fables from the Middle Ages). Lucifer wants to give human beings world-pictures; Ahriman works through abstract world-concepts. Michael wants human beings to understand the world as divine revelation. This is the message of this Michael Letter.

11

How the Michael-forces Work in the Earliest Unfolding of the Consciousness Soul

December 7, 1924

The eleventh Michael Letter returns to the theme of Michael's activity in the centuries preceding the age of the consciousness soul. This time, however, historical events and facts are used to illustrate the character of this twilight period rather than the sagas and fables that were the subject of the previous letter. Yet the stories of Gerhard the Good and Duke Ernst were not an unnecessary excursion into the realm of mythology. Instead, they were a preparation for understanding the enigmatic personality to whom the present letter draws attention: Joan of Arc.

For historians, the Hundred Years' War presents no mysteries. Owing to their succession from William the Conqueror, the kings of England ruled large parts of northern France. When internal dissension weakened the powers of the kings of France, the rulers of England saw it as an open invitation to extend their dominion over the whole of the country. The ensuing war dragged on for more than a century, and the English were well on the way to achieving their aim when things took an unexpected turn. The French rallied and inflicted defeats of such magnitude on the invaders that the

English withdrew and ultimately abandoned all possessions on the other side of the Channel.

It would all appear quite simple if it were not for the fact that the unexpected turn of events was due to one single person, an illiterate peasant girl of seventeen. The appearance of Joan of Arc (1412–31) would, however, not make much sense (and does not make sense in the history books) if one sees in that war no more than one of the many expansionist feuds that are typical of those centuries. What was at stake in the Hundred Years' War was not the size of the English possessions in France but the future evolution of humanity in the age of the consciousness soul. This is the claim Rudolf Steiner makes. It can only be understood if one considers what would have happened without the intervention of Joan of Arc. In this case Britain and France would have become a 'United Kingdom' and this kingdom would have been – as France was to be in the following centuries – heavily involved in the power struggles on the Continent. A commitment of this kind would have effectively prevented Britain from becoming a seafaring nation. It would have prevented the founding of British colonies all over the world.

Nowadays we tend to view the former British Empire as nothing more than a gigantic system of exploitation, and indeed it was that. After all, most of the people who crossed the oceans of the world did so for economic reasons and not out of any philanthropic motives. But what this overlooks are the more far-reaching consequences – quite unintended by the leading figures of empire – that contact with the British had on peoples of other nations, whether as pirates or missionaries, convicts or traders, mercenaries or farmers. What every one of these British adventurers took with them as an innate disposition was a strong sense of personal independence, of personal freedom. It is true that many of them did not wish to instil this sense of freedom in the peoples they dominated and colonised, but they did so anyway simply by being there and coming into contact with them. That such freedom, whether

11. HOW THE MICHAEL-FORCES WORK

political or personal, brings its own problems is a different story. Humanity as a whole is still in the throes of learning this lesson. But what matters is that all over the world there exists the idea of freedom, no matter how distorted, vague or misunderstood it might be. It is an ideal that, in spite of all the errors of the present, will unite humanity in the time to come. This idea of freedom is what has to be developed in the age of the consciousness soul. *The Philosophy of Freedom* had to originate in Germany, but to awaken the instinctive urge toward freedom in all people was the unique task of the British, no matter how imperfectly and problematically they fulfilled this task.

So we have a paradoxical situation in that the British Empire had to come into existence in order to provide something from which the colonised peoples could break free and assert their independence. A second paradox is that England had to be defeated by Joan of Arc in order to subsequently become a worldwide empire. Finally, a third paradox lies in the fact that while Joan of Arc's deed was essential for the development of the consciousness soul, what enabled her to fulfil her task were atavistic clairvoyant forces – her visionary experiences. In other words, Michael used in Joan soul-forces of the past in order to protect and save the soul-forces of the future, the consciousness soul. This is something that could only happen in this twilight era when the old faculties of soul still lingered and the new ones were just beginning to emerge. This half-light that shines in the stories of Gerhard the Good and of Duke Ernst also guided Joan of Arc. But – and this is especially pointed out in this letter – this same muted light, half-dusk, half-dawn, also illuminated the beginning of the Rosicrucian movement.

The books of the alchemists, such as *The Chymical Wedding of Christian Rosenkreutz*, speak in imaginations which the dawning consciousness soul finds baffling and obscure; they refer, however, to natural processes in the world and in human beings. The way in which the above-mentioned book came into existence is characteristic of this epoch. It was written by a young man called Valentin Andrea (1586–1654), who was only eighteen years old at the time. It seems unlikely that he understood what he had written; in later life he became a Protestant minister, wrote boring moralising tracts and rejected the outpourings of his youth. Yet Rudolf Steiner's comments on *The Chymical Wedding* make clear that it describes a Rosicrucian initiation. In short, Valentin Andrea was an instrument just as, in a different context, Joan of Arc was an instrument. Both 'instruments' received their messages when they were around eighteen years old, which, according to the seven-year rhythms in human development described by Steiner, is before 'I'-development begins at twenty-one.

One can see from both instances – from Joan of Arc, who acted boldly and openly in shaping historical events, and from the Rosicrucian brotherhood, which worked in secret behind the scenes of history – that this period of transition from the age of the intellectual soul to the age of the consciousness soul was more difficult and more dangerous than any similar transition in the history of humanity. For the first time in human evolution the hour of freedom had arrived when human beings should find in themselves, through their own forces, the direction towards the future. And Michael, though he was not ruler of the age at the time, nevertheless had to influence events so that when his regency did come, people would be able to find him in the world of thought.

The world of thoughts – by which we organise and understand the world and ourselves – is the sphere in which Michael can be found in the present age. It is therefore quite apposite that in this letter Rudolf Steiner points to the contrast between Joan of Arc, who lived in the transition period, and the French thinker René Descartes (1596–1650), who lived 200 years later, when the consciousness soul had already grown in strength. On other occasions and in other contexts Rudolf Steiner has strongly disagreed with Descartes' fundamental proposition, 'I think, therefore I am'. But in this letter we are

11. HOW THE MICHAEL-FORCES WORK

not concerned with the truth or falsehood of this philosophy. Instead, we must look upon it as a symptom, and as a symptom of the new age nothing could show the human soul's situation more clearly than the bald statement: 'The proof that I really exist lies in the fact that I think.' Not my body, whose functions are outside my consciousness, not my feelings, which are changeable and subjective, nor other people's assurances (they could all be figments of a dream), but only the objective clarity of my own thinking can give me the certainty that my existence is an objective fact. All of this is a poor logical argument, not least because I exist even when I am asleep and do not think at all, but it is a wonderful phenomenon of the time when somebody could feel themselves to be the producer of their own thoughts and regard this activity as proof of their own reality. Neither Plato nor Aristotle could have made such an assertion; for them thoughts were given, not made by human beings.

It might seem an enormous step from the visions of Joan of Arc to the abstract philosophy of Descartes, yet there is a connection. Just as Britain had a part to play in the development of the consciousness soul, so did France. If Joan of Arc had not come to the rescue of the French and if, therefore, France had become an annex of Britain, the specific contribution of French thinkers to European thought – thinkers like Descartes, Pascal, Voltaire and Rousseau – could not have come about. It was in France, after all, that the three great ideals of the consciousness soul were first proclaimed: Liberty, Equality and Fraternity. It is therefore no coincidence that two French nationals figure prominently in this Michael Letter.

12

Hindrances and Helps to the Michael-forces

December 14, 1924

The twelfth Michael Letter speaks again of the historical situation at the beginning of the age of the consciousness soul. We can gain a better understanding of the situation if we draw a comparison with the previous epochs of the post-Atlantean period. In the Egyptian epoch the 'I' worked on the astral body to create the sentient soul; in the Greco-Roman epoch the work of the 'I' was directed toward the etheric body and this gave rise to the intellectual soul. In the present epoch, which began in the fifteenth century, the 'I' works upon the physical body to produce the consciousness soul. In the higher members of the human organisation, in the etheric and astral bodies, there is no death. The forces of death exist only in the physical body and it is this encounter with death that makes the present age – and the development of the consciousness soul – different from previous stages of evolution. This encounter also affects human thinking and human ideas, and this is what is described in this letter.

In the fourteenth and fifteenth centuries, the only people who still had the time and energy to devote to philosophical thought were members of the clergy. It is therefore not surprising that this thinking turned to theological questions, out of which there arose many heated controversies. In fact, these people questioned things that had not been questioned before.

One such a thinker was the English bishop Anselm of Canterbury (1093–1109). He found it necessary to prove by logic that God existed. One can regard him as a forerunner of Descartes, who found it necessary to prove his own existence with his famous dictum, 'I think, therefore I am.' No previous age would have seen any point in proving one's own or God's existence – after all, these were things one knew with certainty. The age of the consciousness soul has no such certainties and Anselm's 'proof' is a symptom of the doubts and insecurities that came with this epoch. The so-called 'ontological proof' of Anselm goes like this: if God exists he must be a perfect being. But a being that lacks the property of existing would not be perfect, and therefore God, since he is perfect, must also exist. Unfortunately for Anselm, one could not even prove logically that giraffes exist. Whether something is or is not is a matter of experience, not of logic.

The same uncertainty lies behind the controversies surrounding the sacrament of Communion. Up to the fifteenth century Christians had taken it for granted that Christ was present in the bread and wine of Communion. Now it was proposed (and later was accepted as doctrine by the Protestant churches) that bread and wine were only symbols and did not contain any spiritual power or reality. Anselm's 'proof' shows that there was no longer the instinctive awareness of the Father God, and the interpretation of Holy Communion as a mere symbol indicates the loss of an instinctive awareness of the Son God, Christ.

This makes another personality mentioned in this letter a figure of special interest. It is the Cardinal Nicholas of Cusa (1401–64). He represents a new certainty, far ahead of his time. The Roman Catholic Church, of which he was a high dignitary, was, and still is, firmly rooted in the mental attitudes of the age of the intellectual soul. When it came under attack by men who

12. HINDRANCES AND HELPS

spoke already with the voice of the consciousness soul, men like John Wycliffe (c. 1330–84) or Jan Hus (c. 1372–1415), it could only respond by condemning them as heretics. Huss was burned at the stake and Wycliffe barely escaped the same fate. Nicholas of Cusa tried to exert a moderating influence in the heated discussions of the Church Councils that dealt with these 'heretics'. It comes almost as a surprise that Nicholas of Cusa himself was never accused of holding heretical views. After all, he was the first man to express the opinion that the earth was a planet like the others and circled round the sun. It was a view he put forward with considerably greater effect in his next incarnation as Copernicus (1473–1543), one of the founders of modern astronomy. However, it was in his life as Cardinal Nicholas of Cusa that he came to an insight that makes him a herald of the Michael impulse. An idea came to him during a sea voyage – an idea that can be summarised in two words: *docta ignorantia*, which means learned or wise ignorance.

In our daily lives we find ourselves preoccupied with this or that question, but no matter what answer we come up with, we are aware that our thinking is something quite unreal compared to the realities of sense experience, to the world around us. What would happen if we stopped thinking? This is exactly what Rudolf Steiner suggests in a lecture given on February 11, 1909. It is a lecture giving instructions for the development of thinking and it contains, paradoxically, the advice that one should regularly, at some point during the day, forbid oneself to form any thought at all. When the self does not think then the force of thinking continues on its own, and these moments of 'not-thinking' are, so Steiner says, especially beneficial for our thinking.

In such moments one does not think about something; instead one experiences thinking itself as a streaming force, as a world-process. It is not the self that is active in this process – forming thoughts, ideas and concepts – but the world. One has the experience: 'Not I think but the world thinks in me.' This is what Nicholas of Cusa experienced. He called it 'ignorance' because our ordinary thinking, normally occupied with purely mundane matters, is temporarily inactive, and he called it 'wise ignorance' for it is a participation in the active, living wisdom of the world. This living wisdom of the world is a manifestation of the third person of the Holy Trinity, the Holy Spirit.

It is in this sense that Rudolf Steiner spoke of thinking as the true communion of humanity.[1] It is a communion with the Holy Spirit. It is also the aim of *The Philosophy of Freedom* to lead to the experience of thinking as a communion. Nicholas of Cusa is a unique personality in that he came, in the fifteenth century, to an experience that belonged properly to the end of the nineteenth century, with the beginning of the Michael Age and the appearance of *The Philosophy of Freedom*.

One can see now in what strange ways Michael had to work during that period of transition. In relation to Joan of Arc he had to use forces that belonged to a previous epoch, whereas in relation to Nicholas of Cusa he had to call on forces whose time had not yet come. This is the reason why Rudolf Steiner calls Michael's activities in that period 'disturbing': Michael's influence in the fourteenth and fifteenth centuries was not in tune with the normal pace of human development. Yet these disturbances were necessary in order to prepare the ground for the coming of the true Michael Age, which began in 1879. But in the fifteenth century, when men had already lost the instinctive connection with God the Father and God the Son, Nicholas of Cusa brought with his 'wise ignorance' the promise of a new communion through God the Holy Spirit.

The problem that faced Michael in the spiritual world in the fourteenth and fifteenth centuries, to work against the conditions that prevailed at the time, existed also for the Rosicrucians here on Earth. They solved it by separating their esoteric life completely from their life and their positions in the outside world. Outwardly they lived as physicians, merchants or artisans in full accord with the conditions of the time. They were, in fact, so well integrated in the society of these centuries that they were unnoticeable. Their esoteric and

12. HINDRANCES AND HELPS

spiritual work went on in complete secrecy. Only some books of an alchemist nature, published anonymously a century later, indicate that there existed such a spiritual movement. The Rosicrucians, too, anticipated the future in their secret spiritual work which was, however, not allowed to flow into outer life at that time. By keeping this work away from the ordinary life of these centuries, the Rosicrucians ensured that there was no interference with the normal pace of human development.

But with the beginning of the Michael Age at the end of the nineteenth century, the time had come for esoteric and spiritual work to flow into everyday life. This is why anthroposophy is not only a particular, contemporary form of esotericism, but has engendered new forms of medicine, education, agriculture and art, and wants to create new social forms too. The secret teaching of the Rosicrucians has been opened to all in such books as *An Outline of Esoteric Science* or *Theosophy*. What was 'out of time' in the fifteenth century is now 'in time'. It is even desperately needed by our time.

13

Michael's Suffering Over Human Evolution Before the Time of His Earthly Activity

December 21, 1924

The letter of December 21 is the last in which Michael stands at the centre of the discussion. There is still one more Michael Letter to come, but there the Michael theme is no longer central: it is subordinated to the theme of the Logos, the Cosmic Word. This letter is therefore Rudolf Steiner's last communication regarding Michael and as such needs to be taken very seriously. In this final picture Michael is shown as filled with *Sorge*, a word that can only be inadequately translated; the nearest English equivalent would be 'grave concern'. In this final message directly concerning Michael, we are allowed an insight into the soul of the great archangel and learn that it is filled with grave concern about human beings in the present time.

We can understand the reasons for this concern if we recall the evolutionary process described in the previous letters. In the most recent stage of evolution, the age of the consciousness soul, the human 'I' has descended into a world that is the finished work of the gods but in which no divine being is present any longer. Only in this world can the human being develop a personal intelligence and, through intelligence, come to the experience of freedom. Yet this intelligence, gained through beholding a world in which there is nothing divine, cannot tell the human 'I' anything about the divine nature and origin of this 'I'. It is a paradoxical situation: the intelligence that makes us free human beings at the same time blinds us to our own true nature.

In this situation it would seem that the human soul has only two choices. It can let itself be guided by intelligence, which, inevitably, must lead to a materialistic conception of the world and of human beings. Or it can try to hold on to the old instinctive connection with the spiritual world, a connection sustained through the life of feeling. A healthy feeling will indeed assure us that there is a divine world order and that our own being is part of it. But this also means turning our back on intelligence and not using the forces of the consciousness soul, the very forces upon which the future evolution of humanity depends. The path of intelligence confronts us with the danger of uncompromising materialism, and this is the direction in which Ahriman wants to take us; the path of feeling is a flight into the past, and this is the direction in which Lucifer would lead us.

The first few centuries of the age of the consciousness soul show, as Rudolf Steiner demonstrates in this letter, a strong Luciferic trend. The art of the Renaissance was, as the name implies, a revival of the artistic aims of Greece and Rome. Here was a new impulse, but it let itself be guided by religious tradition and the aesthetics of the past. To take another example, when Shakespeare wanted to show elemental beings on the stage in *A Midsummer Night's Dream*, he had to bring in Oberon and Titania, figures who belong to a more ancient tradition. Even Goethe admitted that the images he had used for the closing scenes of *Faust* had their source in the traditions of the Roman Catholic Church. In order to present spiritual realities, artists used images and ideas that came from the past, and the force that infused the traditional elements with new life came from an instinctive feeling within the soul, not from the intellect and not from the forces of the consciousness soul.

13. MICHAEL'S SUFFERING

On the other hand there were people whose work grew out of the new forces of the consciousness soul. The physician William Harvey (1578–1657), who discovered the circulation of the blood and declared the heart to be a mechanical pump, was just such a man. So too was Sir Isaac Newton (1643–1727), who explained the orbits of the planets in terms of the 'law of universal gravitation', and Charles Darwin (1809–82), who declared that natural selection was sufficient to explain the evolution of human beings from simple, single-celled organisms.

This is the situation that causes Michael such grave concern: where a connection with the spiritual world still exists in human beings, it relies upon forces of the past, on faculties of feeling, whereas the forces upon which the future depends, the forces of intelligence as developed by the consciousness soul, are only used in a materialistic, mechanical sense. It is a split that exists in every one of us. The conviction that we belong to a spiritual world arises from the depth of our feeling, but our intelligence, our thinking, does not convey any assurance that we are immortal spirits, it can only deal with practical and material questions. This is true even among anthroposophists: few of us, I doubt, accepted Rudolf Steiner's teaching only after a long, sober and thorough study of his work – it was a feeling that made the decision for us. It is right that this should be so, but if we remain at this initial feeling stage in our connection to anthroposophy, we will not have used the forces of the consciousness soul. We use these forces in our intelligence in daily practical life, but this form of intelligence is not capable of penetrating to the mysteries of the spirit. After all, this intelligence was developed in connection with the finished work of the gods, the natural world around us, and in this form it cannot comprehend the living world of forces and beings that exist above the static, finished work.

It is necessary that this utilitarian intelligence, this intelligence of the finished work, be transformed, not merely for personal reasons, such as to gain a better understanding of Rudolf Steiner's books, but because the world needs a different *kind* of intelligence. It is precisely this utilitarian intelligence that is responsible for the climate crisis, for the social ills of our time, and for the technological innovations that have impoverished human beings. This intelligence is not something neutral but a destructive force like an infectious disease. The fact that it is fostered in schools and universities, that science, art and politics are dominated by it, constitutes the great sickness of our time. This is the cause of Michael's grave concern, and it prompts the question that stands before him: will humanity be able to transform this utilitarian intelligence, this intelligence of the finished work?

Since the transformation of intelligence is also a transformation from thinking in abstract concepts to thinking in pictures, it is justified to use the images of an old legend for the situation in which humanity finds itself today. It is an episode from Chapter 21 of the book of Numbers in the Old Testament. During their long journey to the Promised Land, the children of Israel grew weary of their endless wandering through the desert, and they voiced their discontent and unwillingness to put up with the hardships Yahweh had imposed on them. Yahweh's retribution was swift. He sent snakes to attack the grumbling tribes in great numbers; their bites were painful and many people died. Now the children of Israel cried for mercy and Moses prayed to Yahweh to lift the curse he had sent. Yahweh commanded Moses to make a serpent of brass and to raise it up on a pole. Those who had been bitten by the snakes and looked on the serpent would be healed. Moses obeyed, and those who had been made ill by the poisonous snakes and looked on the brass serpent raised up on the pole regained their health.

In this legend the snake appears in two forms. The crawling snakes are poisonous and bring illness and death, but the snake raised up – raised to a higher level – has the power to heal. In the snake crawling on the ground we can recognise a symbol of the intelligence that works destructively, that is bound to the

13. MICHAEL'S SUFFERING

material world, but when it is transformed and raised to higher levels, like the brass serpent lifted up on the pole, it becomes a healing force.

But there is something else hidden in this story from the Old Testament, a secret message. It would not be enough to tell us that intelligence has to be raised to a higher level; we also need to know what it is that can enable us to bring about such a transformation. This too is conveyed by the legend. In Hebrew, the original language of the Old Testament, there are two words for snake. One of these words is *nachash,* and this is used for the poisonous snakes that bring pain and death. Incidentally, the same word is used for the snake that tempted Adam and Eve in the Garden of Eden. *Nachash* is the snake, the intelligence, that makes human beings evil, but which also makes us free. For the brass serpent raised high on the pole, the Old Testament uses another word, *seraph*. The plural form of this word is the name of the highest hierarchy, the Seraphim.

Seraphim, Cherubim and Thrones make up the First Hierarchy, the hierarchy of the Father God. They are the beings who are in the immediate presence of the Trinity, the source and origin of all there is. The Seraphim are the highest rank of these exalted spirits and thus nearest to God. Rudolf Steiner calls them the 'Spirits of Love'. The brass serpent, the snake that has the power to heal, to bring health and harmony, is a Seraph, a Spirit of Love. We find this healing serpent also in Greek and Roman mythology. Two snakes winding themselves around the staff of Mercury are still today the symbol of the healing professions. And the Green Snake that brings Goethe's fairy tale to a happy conclusion through an act of self-sacrifice has the same meaning: the healing power of love.

What makes our ordinary thinking, our ordinary intelligence, a destructive force, akin to the *nachash* snakes of the Old Testament, is the absence of love. To be sure, we can have this cold, reptilian thinking in our heads and somewhere else in our soul a vast amount of sentimental warmth, but this is not what the symbol of the raised serpent is meant to convey.

It calls on us to develop a thinking that is at the same time a form of love: a thinking that is as free of personal sentiment as pure mathematics, but which treats ideas and concepts with the same tender care with which we might treat the young plants in our garden. In a lecture given on January 1, 1919,[1] Rudolf Steiner said of this thinking that the mere content of spiritual science is not the most important part of our study. What matters is the way in which we have to think in order to understand spiritual science. It is a thinking that is radically different from the usual thinking that analyses, dissects and dismembers. It is a thinking that synthesises and builds up. This is the reason why there is in spiritual science such an emphasis on the Christ impulse, because the Christ impulse lies in the direction of this thinking.

In another lecture Steiner gave, this one on February 6, 1917, he said:

> It is far more important that we learn through spiritual science to have an inner discourse in our thoughts with the spiritual world than to acquire theoretical thoughts.[2]

This is what the symbol of the raised serpent is meant to convey and also what the Green Snake in Goethe's fairy tale is meant to convey: that our thinking should become an intimate conversation, a thought-conversation, with the spiritual world. That fairy tale, whose real hero is the Green Snake, was an inspiration Goethe received from Michael. It is Michael himself who speaks to us through the fairy tale, and it is again Michael who speaks to us through these letters. In this last message he makes us aware of the question that causes him grave concern: will human beings do what they are meant to do and transform the earthbound intelligence?

The Leading Thoughts (of which the 'Michael Letters' form a part) begin with the following sentence: 'Anthroposophy is a path of knowledge, to guide the spiritual in the human being to the spiritual in the universe.'[3] If this wording were

13. MICHAEL'S SUFFERING

not intentional it would be one of the clumsiest metaphors in Rudolf Steiner's work. Imagine somebody saying that Princes Street guides us from the West End to the East End. A road or a path leads from A to B, it does not 'guide' us there. But the reason Rudolf Steiner says this particular path seeks to 'guide' is that this path is not made of earth and stones but is a being. This being wants something: to guide the spirit of the human being to the spirit of the universe. It is a description of Michael.

14

A Christmas Contemplation: The Mystery of the Logos

December 28, 1924

The last of the letters in which the name of Michael occurs bears the title 'A Christmas Contemplation' and the subtitle 'A Logos Mystery'. The headings already indicate that from here onwards the Michael Mystery is no longer the subject of the discussion, but rather the Logos or Christ Mystery.

In this letter Rudolf Steiner compares three rhythms as they find expression in the activities of three spiritual beings. The first is Michael, who becomes the Time Spirit every two thousand years or so. In this role he descends from spiritual heights to regions close to the Earth – the elemental or astral world – before ascending again to Devachan, which is his proper sphere. But he never descends all the way to the physical plane. Michael is never on the Earth itself. This is in complete contrast to the Earth Spirit, who lives in the yearly rhythm of rising into the cosmos in the summer and withdrawing into the Earth in the winter, and whose sphere is, of course, the Earth. Between the Earth Spirit and Michael, there is Christ, the Logos, who incarnated once and once only in a physical body but who has forever since made the Earth his sphere of activity.

Steiner follows this comparison with a comparison between Christ and the Earth Spirit. Here it becomes necessary to understand something of this rather mysterious being called the Earth Spirit. When we use the word 'Nature' to encompass the phenomena of the mineral, plant and animal worlds surrounding us, it is a complete abstraction. But in the early Middle Ages there were still people, such as the wise monks of Chartres, for whom the goddess Natura was a reality. In ancient Greece the same being was known as Persephone, the daughter of the goddess Demeter. It was said that Persephone spent one half of the year with the gods of the upperworld, the cosmos, who were her kinfolk, and the other half with her husband, Hades, the god of the underworld. In this myth we can recognise an imagination for the yearly rhythm of the Earth Spirit mentioned above.

This yearly ascent and descent has a function; it is necessary for the natural world around us. As we have learned from the previous Michael Letters, although the natural world is the finished work of the gods, they are no longer present in it. But this finished work could not last, could not go on existing, if it did not receive renewing forces from the cosmos. The elemental beings of the plant world would become lifeless shadows without the regenerating forces of the spirit. The being who brings these forces into the finished work is Persephone, the goddess Natura. One can therefore say that what Persephone does for the beings of Nature is similar to what Christ does for human beings. But Persephone's deed has to be repeated every year, while Christ's deed was done once and for all time at the Mystery of Golgotha.

But this still leaves the question, what kind of being is Persephone? Rudolf Steiner speaks quite often of the Earth Spirit or Earth Soul but gives only hints with regard to the nature of this being. One such hint can be found in a lecture given on January 2, 1914, in Leipzig. There Steiner makes a reference to the name of Yahweh or Jehovah, the God of the Old Testament.[1]

If we want to pursue this hint further, we must keep in mind that this name, and even the letters forming this name, are regarded by the Jews with utmost reverence. There even existed an esoteric school that perceived profound occult wisdom in the word Yahweh, but the name was not written down the way it is now in modern languages. It was written Y-H-V-H, leaving out the vowels, as is still the custom in Hebrew. The first letter, Y (or J), was said to represent the male element and the following letters, H-V-H, the female element in Yahweh. Yahweh is the Moon-god and, as the Moon forces rule reproduction, he is both male and female.

We know from *An Outline of Esoteric Science* that at an early stage of Earth evolution the Moon and the Earth were one body. But the substance of this planetary body hardened to such a degree that human souls became less and less able to incarnate in this substance. Yahweh gathered these hardening forces and departed with them from the Earth. Out of them he formed the Moon, which became his domain, his cosmic fortress, and from there he continued to work on the evolution of humanity.

But not all of the forces of Yahweh were withdrawn from the Earth. It was only the male element, represented by the letter Y (or J), that made its abode on the Moon. The female part, represented by the letters H-V-H, remained on Earth. In Hebrew, H-V-H is 'Hava' or, as we pronounce it, 'Eva' and means 'the mother of life'. Hava, Eva or Eve, the female counterpart to Yahweh, is the Earth Spirit, the one whom the Greeks called Persephone and the teachers of Chartres called the goddess Natura. When biodynamic farmers find a close connection between plant life and the positions of the Moon, they are only discovering the esoteric truth that the Earth Spirit, the mother of life, is related to the Moon-god, Yahweh.

The separation between the male and female elements in Yahweh also brought about corresponding changes in the nature of human beings. Before this separation human beings, who had been created 'in the image of God', were, like Yahweh, both male and female – this is also stated in the Old Testament.[2] After the separation, humanity too was divided into man and woman. The biblical Adam and Eve represent this division. Adam is the physical expression of the spirit whose abode is the Moon; Eve (or Eva) is the physical representative of the Earth Spirit whose name she bears.

The division of the sexes is not merely a physical matter, it has spiritual significance too. When a child is born they receive from their parents two opposite yet complementary tendencies. From the father come the forces that work towards individualism, towards making each human being specific and unique. From the mother comes the tendency towards integration, towards making the individual a part of a larger unit, part of a community. Every human being has both tendencies, and their reconciliation is an important part of our karma. The forces of individualism go back to Adam and to the Moon Spirit; the forces of integration to Eva and the Earth Spirit.

However, as we know, Yahweh could only prepare humanity for the coming of the Sun Spirit, Christ, who can restore to human souls the perfect harmony between the forces of separation and integration. In the lectures on the Gospel of Luke, Rudolf Steiner indicates that the Adam-being played an important part in preparing human beings for the Mystery of Golgotha.[3] This Adam-being had been incarnated as the prophet Elijah and was again incarnated in John the Baptist. But if we find Adam in the environment of Christ Jesus we might also ask if the Eva-being was connected with the events surrounding the Mystery of Golgotha.

It is a characteristic feature of Rudolf Steiner's work that he reveals certain secrets but not others. He leaves us in the dark about some things, as if to say we should find them out for ourselves. As was mentioned above, one of the things he never stated directly is the nature of the Earth Spirit. There is the reference to Persephone in the last Michael Letter, and there is the hint about a connection with Yahweh quoted before, but nothing is said outright. There is a similar reticence with regard to a certain aspect of the two Jesus children.

14. A CHRISTMAS CONTEMPLATION

One of the two Jesus boys is the reincarnation of Zarathustra, a very highly developed individuality. The other Jesus boy is the 'Heavenly Adam', the innocent soul of all humanity, in whom love, not wisdom, is the content of the soul. Here we find once again the two tendencies mentioned previously. The reincarnated Zarathustra represents the forces of individualism in their highest form. The other Jesus child expresses with his whole being the forces that achieve the highest integration: divine, selfless love for all humanity.

Concerning the mother of the Zarathustra-Jesus, Steiner said that what lived in her was the Cosmic Wisdom, Sophia. He gave no corresponding communication about the mother of the other Jesus child. We are told only that she died young but her soul united itself with the Sophia-mother at the baptism of Jesus in the River Jordan. Who was this being who was worthy to give birth to the loving soul of all humanity and who could, when she had left the physical body, unite herself with the being called Sophia? It could only be she who is the bearer of the Earth-wisdom: Eve, Eva, Hava, the mother of life, the one who is also called Persephone and the goddess Natura.

This being lives in the world that is the finished work of the gods and she brings into this world forces of renewal from the cosmos. Without these life-giving forces the Earth would cease to provide human beings with the possibility of physical existence, and if this happened human beings would be unable to develop as free beings. The forces that are hostile to the mission of Earth have their outer expression in the frost and darkness of winter. Yet it is just when the winter forces seem to gain the upper hand, in the darkest time of the year, that the Earth Spirit bestows on all creatures new life forces from the cosmos. This is what was celebrated as the festival of the Winter Solstice all over the Earth, long before Christianity. And the ancient wisdom also recognised that the spirit who renewed life in Nature also lived in the social instincts of human beings, in the wish for togetherness. This is also the meaning of the message that the shepherds heard in the Gospel of Luke: 'Peace on earth to all human beings of goodwill.' Earth itself is the source of this instinctive good will.

However, the conscious impulse to work towards the brotherhood of all human beings could not come from the Earth Spirit, who is, as we have seen, part of the Moon-god Yahweh. The conscious impulse had to come from the Sun Spirit, Christ. When we celebrate the birth of Jesus, we pay homage to the harmony of the Sun and Moon forces, of conscious will and deep human instinct. This is the magic of Christmas when it is celebrated in the right spirit: it calls up feelings from the depth of our souls and, at the same time, places before us a conscious ideal – human brotherhood.

But we can only move towards this great ideal if we overcome and transform the forces that have their outward manifestation in the frost of winter: the cold intellect. Our kindest feelings, our most deeply felt compassion, cannot prevent the drift toward disaster, cannot cure the ills of our time unless there is a transformation in our thinking. This is why we need the Michael impulse. Now we can see why Rudolf Steiner, in this Christmas message, the last he gave in his life on Earth, speaks of three beings: Michael, Christ and Persephone.

References

1. At the Dawn of the Michael Age
1. See for instance lecture of Aug 11, 1924 in *True and False Paths of Spiritual Research* (CW 243) Rudolf Steiner Press, UK 2020.
2. *Anthroposophical Leading Thoughts,* (CW 26) Rudolf Steiner Press, UK 2012, p. 13.

2. The Condition of the Human Soul
1. See Matt 25:14–30 and Luke 19:11–27.
2. See for instance *The Tensions Between East and West* (CW 83) Anthroposophic Press, USA 1983, p. 50.
3. From the Michaelmas seasonal prayer of the Act of Consecration of Man.

3. The Way of Michael and What Preceded It
1. See lecture of Jan 10, 1915 in *Artistic Sensitivity* (CW 161) SteinerBooks, USA 2018.
2. See lecture of Sep 28, 1924 in *Karmic Relationships,* Vol IV (CW 238) Rudolf Steiner Press, UK 1997.
3. See lecture of May 7, 1921 in *Colour* (CW 291) Rudolf Steiner Press, UK 2005.
4. *Man in the Light of Occultism, Theosophy and Philosophy* (CW 137) Rudolf Steiner Press, UK 1964, p. 7.
5. *Anthroposophical Leading Thoughts,* p. 69.
6. See lecture of Oct 8, 1923 in *Nine Lectures on Bees* (CW 351) Anthroposophic Press, USA 1998.

4. Michael's Task in the Sphere of Ahriman
1. *Christ and the Spiritual World and the Search for the Holy Grail* (CW 149) Rudolf Steiner Press, UK 2008, pp. 99f.
2. *Karmic Relationships,* Vol VI (CW 240) Rudolf Steiner Press, UK 1989, p. 158.
3. ibid, pp. 171f.
4. *Study of Man* (CW 293) Rudolf Steiner Press, UK 2011, p. 190.

5: The Experiences of Michael in the Course of His Cosmic Mission
1. See lecture of April 14, 1909 in *The Spiritual Hierarchies and the Physical World* (CW 110) SteinerBooks, USA 2008.
2. *Concerning the Astral World and Devachan* (CW 88) SteinerBooks, USA 2018, p. 184.

6. The Activity of Michael and the Future of Humanity

1. For 'Hymn of the Pearl' see 'Acts of Thomas' in: Elliot, J K, *The Apocryphal New Testament*, Oxford University Press, Oxford 2009.
2. *The Spiritual Guidance of the Individual and Humanity* (CW 15) Anthroposophic Press, USA 1991, p.62.

7. The Michael-Christ Experience of Humanity

1. See for instance lecture of Feb 11, 1907 in *Esoteric Lessons 1904–1909* (CW 266/1) SteinerBooks, USA 2007.

8. Michael's Mission in the Cosmic Age of Human Freedom

1. See lecture of April 12, 1917 in *Building Stones for an Understanding of the Mystery of Golgotha* (CW 175) Rudolf Steiner Press, UK 2015.
2. See lecture of Nov 22, 1914 in *Our Connection with the Elemental World: The World as the Result of Balancing Influences* (CW 158) Rudolf Steiner Press, UK 2016.
3. See, for example, 1 Corinthians 13.

9. World-thoughts in the Working of Michael

1. See lecture of August 4, 1924 in *Karmic Relationships,* Vol III (CW 237) Rudolf Steiner Press, UK 1977.
2. ibid, lecture of Aug 8, 1924, p. 167.

12. Hindrances and Helps to the Michael-forces

1. See for instance Chapter 10 in *The Story of my Life* (CW 28) SteinerBooks, USA 2006.

13. Michael's Suffering Over Human Evolution

1. See lecture of January 1, 1919 in *How Can Humanity Find the Christ Again?* (CW 187) Anthroposophic Press, USA 1984.
2. *Building Stones for an Understanding of the Mystery of Golgotha,* p. 15.
3. *Anthroposophical Leading Thoughts*, p. 13.

14. A Christmas Contemplation: The Mystery of the Logos

1. *Christ and the Spiritual World and the Search for the Holy Grail* (CW 149) Rudolf Steiner Press, UK 2008, p. 118f.
2. See Gen 1:27.
3. *The Gospel of Luke* (CW 114), Rudolf Steiner Press, UK 1988.

Further Reading

Steiner, Rudolf, *Philosophy, Cosmology and Religion* (CW 215), Anthroposophic Press, USA 1984.
—, *The Philosophy of Freedom* (CW 4), Rudolf Steiner Press, UK 2011.
—, *The Riddles of Philosophy* (CW 18), SteinerBooks, USA 2009.
—, *True and False Paths of Spiritual Research* (CW 243) Rudolf Steiner Press, UK 2020.

Index

Alexander the Great 16
Andrea, Valentin 87f
Angelus Silesius 46
Anselm of Canterbury 92
Aquinas, Thomas 14
astrology 56f

Babylonian civilisation 11

Chymical Wedding of Christian Rosenkreutz 87
colour 64
Copernicus, Nicholas 93
Cosmic Intelligence 11f, 73, 75, 77

Darwin, Charles 99
Demeter 106
Descartes, René 88

Empedocles 12
Ernst, Duke 82f
Eschenbach, Wolfram von 38
Eve 107–9

Freemasons 62

Gerhard the Good 80f
Goethe 38f, 64
—, fairy tale 38, 40–42, 102
Greco-Roman civilisation 12

Harvey, William 99
Heraclitus 12, 33
Hundred Years' War 85f
Hus, Jan 93
Hymn of the Pearl 54

Isis 54

Jacob, patriarch 24–26
Jesuits 62

Joan of Arc 86f, 89, 94

Marduk 11
Moses 100

Natura (goddess) 106, 109
Newton, Isaac 99
Nicholas of Cusa 92–94
Nominalists 13
Novalis 54

Odysseus 24

Parable of the Talents 20
Parsifal 38
Paul, St 70
Persephone 106, 109
philosophy 30
pietà 37–40

Realists 14
Rosicrucians 87f, 94

Scholasticism 13
serpent 100f
Snow White 32f
Solomon, King 25
stepmother 31f

tailor, little 47–49
Talents, Parable of the 20
Thales 12, 33
Thomas Aquinas 14
Tiamat, dragon 11

Valentin Andrea 88

Wolfram von Eschenbach 38
Wycliffe, John 93

Yahweh 69–71, 107

You may also be interested in...

The Apocalypse in Rudolf Steiner's Lecture Series

Charles Kovacs

In 1908, Rudolf Steiner gave a series of lectures about the Book of Revelation. He showed that the messages to the seven churches and the unsealing of the seven seals should be understood as references to initiation. In this light, the great images of the Apocalypse take on new meaning.

In this book, illustrated with his own colour paintings, Charles Kovacs helps us make sense of the apocalyptic imagery, including the four beasts, the four riders, the woman clothed with the sun, and the New Jerusalem.

florisbooks.co.uk

The Spiritual Background to Christian Festivals

Charles Kovacs

The rhythms of the earth can be seen in, for example, the daily cycle of day and night, or in the changing seasons. Rudolf Steiner spoke about how Christian festivals such as Easter, Whitsun and Christmas fitted not just into these patterns, but also into larger cosmic rhythms and, on a smaller scale, human rhythms.

In this concise book Charles Kovacs explores the structure of our calendar year and looks in detail at the background to each Christian festival, including lesser-known ones such as St John's Tide and Michaelmas.

florisbooks.co.uk

Christianity and the Ancient Mysteries

Reflections on Rudolf Steiner's Christianity as Mystical Fact

Charles Kovacs

Charles Kovacs brings his deep knowledge of esoteric writings, mythology and Steiner's lectures to show how the way for Christianity was prepared in the ancient pre-Christian mysteries of Egypt and Greece. He discusses the symbolic and real events of the gospels, as well as looking at some of the understandings and disputes of the early Christians.

florisbooks.co.uk

Waldorf education books by Charles Kovacs

Class 4 (age 9–10)
    Norse Mythology

Classes 4 and 5 (age 9–11)
    The Human Being and the Animal World

Classes 5 and 6 (age 10–12)
    Ancient Greece
    Botany

Class 6 (age 11–12)
    Ancient Rome

Classes 6 and 7 (age 11–13)
    Geology and Astronomy

Class 7 (age 12–13)
    The Age of Discovery

Classes 7 and 8 (age 12–14)
    Muscles and Bones

Class 8 (age 13–14)
    The Age of Revolution

Class 11 (age 16–17)
    Parsifal and the Search for the Grail

florisbooks.co.uk

Rudolf Steiner and The Christian Community

Peter Selg

The relationship between The Christian Community and the Anthroposophical Society is complex and often misunderstood. In this unique book Peter Selg examines key questions about Rudolf Steiner's intentions for The Christian Community.

This long-overdue book is a significant exploration of Steiner's legacy which should have far-reaching implications for mutual understanding and cooperation between The Christian Community and the wider anthroposophical world.

florisbooks.co.uk

The Lord's Prayer and Rudolf Steiner

Peter Selg

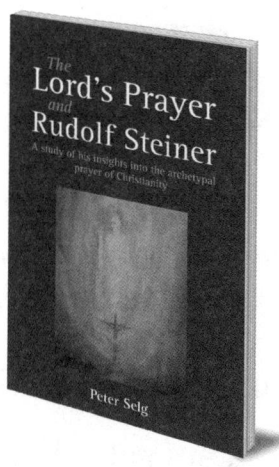

Rudolf Steiner once called the Lord's Prayer the 'greatest initiation prayer', and he spoke about it many times, also referring to it as the central prayer of Christian experience.

This book is, however, the first time that all of Steiner's comments, accounts and perspectives have been brought together in one place, presenting the full scope and depth of his ideas. Along the way, Peter Selg reveals some surprising insights into the spiritual history and mission of Christianity.

florisbooks.co.uk

For news on all our **latest books**,
and to receive **exclusive discounts**,
join our mailing list at:

florisbooks.co.uk

Plus subscribers get a FREE book
with every online order!

We will never pass your details to anyone else.